BEFORE
THE BOOTH

BEFORE
THE BOOTH

D. JAY MARTIN, EDITOR

MORNING JOY MEDIA
POTTSTOWN, PENNSYLVANIA

Published by Morning Joy Media.

Visit morningjoymedia.com for more information on bulk discounts and special promotions, or e-mail your questions to info@morningjoymedia.com.

D. Jay Martin's Photo: Kristen Sigourney
Essay Sketches: Shannon Vining
Design: Debbie Capeci
Pastoral Reading Team: Tim Doering, Brandon Hanks
Design Advisors: Dan Desrosiers, Tim Gruber
Cover Images: Adobe Stock

ISBN 978-1-937107-75-8 (paperback)

ISBN 978-1-937107-76-5 (ebook)

Printed in the United States of America

CONTENTS

FOREWORD

TIM DOERING
Founder of Netzer

ONE OF GOD'S ETERNAL PLANS, according to Ephesians 3, is to display his multifaceted wisdom through his church. Jesus' redemption offers the opportunity to bring humanity's diversity into a reconciled community where the fuller council of God can be discerned and voiced together. While this is only possible because of the gospel, practically forming these relationships takes effort and intentionality. Ephesians 4 tells us that living into this calling takes great humility and patience. This book is possible because of many leaders choosing for years to honor and connect with one another across the body of Christ.

As someone centrally focused on seeing Christ glorified through the unity of the church, this project thrills me. As someone passionate about the people of God being mutually equipped by the breadth of the knowledge of God across the church, I celebrate this discipleship resource. Finally, as one who spends a great deal of time working with pastors and leaders, I am so grateful for these women and men of God who have chosen, amid all the demands of life and ministry, to collaborate for the greater good of the kingdom of God. Our King is honored by your work. I cannot think of one better positioned to pull this all together than D. Jay Martin. Much of this is possible directly due to your willingness to walk in the humility of Jesus. We honor the work of Christ in you, Pastor D. Jay (Philippians 2:1–4).

INTRODUCTION

D. JAY MARTIN

Pastor of Leadership & Vision at Parker Ford Church

IN THE GARDEN OF GETHSEMANE, hours before his death, Jesus prayed that his followers would be one: "Now protect them ... so that they will be united just as we are" (John 17:11 NLT). This is the heart of Jesus for his bride.

Perhaps like me, you have been discouraged by Christians tearing one another apart over partisan politics. As followers of Jesus, we are citizens of heaven, kingdom ambassadors, and disciples of Christ. We have been entrusted by God to carry on Christ's ongoing ministry of reconciliation!

I've been a lead pastor for a little over ten years, and the past decade of pastoral ministry has been framed in large part by the insanity and division of contemporary American partisan politics. Invariably, during each political cycle, many good-hearted, earnest Christians get riled up, tripped up, and misled by the voices of fear and fear-mongering in both the media and by politicians and political agents. This fear seeps into families and into churches, causing division and hurt among the people of God.

How tragic. And how utterly unnecessary.

We are not a people of fear. We are a people of the King. Earthly politics are important, but they are not the main thing. While I believe it is possible for a Christian to express his or her faith through political engagement, it is also impossible for a Christian to express faith solely through earthly politics. Christians are not a voting bloc. We are foreigners, living in a foreign land, seeking to represent the values, goals, and mission of our King and his kingdom.

This is why I asked a group of my friends and ministry peers who all serve and lead various Christian churches and ministries in Pottstown, Pennsylvania—the town where I serve and lead—to contribute a chapter to a collaborative book called *Before the Booth*. My vision for the book was simple, pastoral, and practical. I wanted to help create a resource designed to help Christians prepare spiritually for the election cycle.

The list of authors includes sixteen pastors and ministry leaders—women and men, folks from the Gen-Z, Millennial, Gen-X, and Baby Boomer generations, Black, White, Asian-American, and Latino, representing ten churches from various denominations and six parachurch ministries operating in the greater Pottstown, Pennsylvania, area. Each author provides their perspective on timeless biblical principles aimed at helping to align the soul of the church with the heart of Jesus during this politically divisive time.

As a pastor, I am not interested in telling you who to vote for in an earthly election. Your ultimate vote belongs to Jesus. That issue was settled when you became a Christian. However, I am deeply passionate about Christians accurately representing the heart of Jesus, especially in the way we treat one another and interact with those outside the faith. After all, as comes up over and over in the book, each human being—no matter who they vote for—is created in the image and likeness of God.

This book is designed to be read individually or as a group *before* you head to the polling station to cast your vote. By all means, vote! But do so first and always as a follower of Jesus. Each chapter of the book includes discussion questions to help facilitate meaningful conversations that point our souls back to Jesus.

May our hearts remain loyal to Jesus alone. He is the only one who can save us and the only one worthy of our complete allegiance.

JESUS IS NEITHER REPUBLICAN NOR DEMOCRAT

TERRANCE PAUL

Lead Pastor of Fresh Start Ministries International

HAVE YOU EVER HEARD SOMEONE confidently declare, "If Jesus were alive today, he would definitely vote for . . ."? In the current political landscape, it is increasingly common for individuals to align their faith with a particular political party. Sometimes, people take it even further and assertively proclaim that Jesus *is* a Republican, or that he *is* a Democrat.

The values modeled perfectly in the life and teachings of Jesus should give any discerning Christian a major clue that Jesus does not fit within the box of partisan politics. As a pastor, community leader, and follower of Christ, I believe it is crucial for us to remember that Jesus transcends political affiliations and cannot be confined to the ideologies of any single human political party.

Partisan politics create a hazardous situation for Christians to navigate. We are pulled between our Christian values and the complexities of the American political process. Followers of Jesus are called to be actively engaged in the world and to seek justice and righteousness. This has led many Christians to participate in the political process. Depending on the needs of our community, as well as the unique passions that the Lord places on our hearts, this can result in a person aligning with one political party or ideology. Christians engaging in the American political process can often be a good thing and a natural extension of our faith.

However, as we attempt to navigate through these complexities, it is important for us to consider the reality that Christians are a diverse group, and, even within the historic orthodox Christian faith, we possess a wide range of theological beliefs *and* political convictions. While some of us may find ourselves aligned with a particular party based on their expressed values and priorities, other faithful Christians may find it difficult to fully embrace that same party, or any one political ideology at all. Because the glory and goodness of Jesus transcend what any human political party can represent, our faith should transcend politics and must not be reduced to a partisan agenda.

It is important for us to approach politics with discernment and humility. We should be guided by biblical principles and the leading of the Holy Spirit rather than blind loyalty to one party. We ought to be open to dialogue and respectful engagement with those who hold different views, seeking to find common ground and work toward the common good.

As Christians we should constantly be reminding ourselves that our allegiance is not to a political party or ideology, but to Christ and his kingdom. This means that we must prioritize what Jesus prioritizes, namely, love, justice, and righteousness in all aspects of our lives. By doing so, we can be a positive influence in the political sphere, working toward a more just and compassionate society.

When we consider Jesus' teachings and example we are provided with a different perspective, one that emphasizes love, compassion, justice, and the kingdom of God above all else. Jesus calls Christians to a higher standard of living than either political party can offer. What follows are some of the most important reasons why I believe that neither the Republican nor the Democratic party can fully represent Jesus.

JESUS PREACHED THE KINGDOM OF GOD, NOT AN EARTHLY KINGDOM

Before Jesus ascended into heaven his disciples asked him if the time had come for Christ to restore the earthly kingdom of Israel. Jesus' response told the disciples that they were asking the wrong question. "He said to them: 'It is not for you to know the times or dates the Father has set by his own authority. But you will receive power when the Holy Spirit comes on you; and you will be my witnesses in Jerusalem, and in all Judea and Samaria, and to the ends of the earth" (Acts 1:7–8). Our focus as disciples of Jesus is to witness to the good news of Jesus.

Jesus consistently spoke about the kingdom of God, which is a realm that surpasses earthly politics and divisions. His kingdom is not bound by any human constructs but rather is founded on principles of love, righteousness, and justice for all. Jesus emphasized that his kingdom is not of this world, and therefore, his teachings cannot be reduced to the agenda of any political party.

Now after John was put in prison, *Jesus came to Galilee, preaching the gospel of the kingdom of God.* (Mark 1:14 NKJV, emphasis added)

JESUS PREACHED COMPASSION AND CARE FOR THE MARGINALIZED

Jesus' ministry showed great care for the marginalized, the oppressed, and the vulnerable. His ministry was characterized by reaching out to the poor and healing the sick. Jesus advocated for the voiceless, the left out, the left back, and the left behind. As followers of Christ, we are called to emulate his compassion and prioritize the needs of the marginalized above any political agenda.

There is no more compelling argument for this than the passage in Matthew 25 when Jesus describes the actions of those welcomed into his Father's kingdom:

> For I was hungry and you gave me something to eat, I was thirsty and you gave me something to drink, I was a stranger and you invited me in, I needed clothes and you clothed me, I was sick and you looked after me, I was in prison and you came to visit me . . . Truly I tell you, whatever you did for one of the least of these brothers and sisters of mine, you did for me. (Matthew 25:35–36, 40)

JESUS VALUED HUMAN DIGNITY

Jesus consistently taught the inherent worth and dignity of every human being. He showed love and respect to all, regardless of their social status, ethnicity, background, or political persuasion. Jesus loved and discipled Matthew the tax collector (who worked with the Romans) as well as Simon the Zealot (who rebelled against the Romans). This value for human dignity should guide our political engagement, ensuring that our actions and policies affirm and uplift the worth of every individual—no matter how much we may disagree with their politics.

> What is man that You are mindful of him, And the son of man that You visit him? For You have made him a little lower than the angels, And You have crowned him with glory and honor. You have made him to have dominion over the works of Your hands; You have put all things under his feet. (Psalm 8:4–6 NKJV)

JESUS PREACHED JUSTICE AND MERCY

Jesus was an advocate for justice and mercy. He often challenged the systems of oppression and called for a society rooted in righteousness. As followers of Christ, we should seek justice for all people, working toward a society that reflects God's desire for fairness and equality.

> Woe to you, scribes and Pharisees, hypocrites! For you pay tithe of mint and anise and cumin, and have neglected the weightier matters of the law: justice and mercy and faith. These you ought to have done, without leaving the others undone. (Matthew 23:23 NKJV)

> He has shown you, O mortal, what is good. And what does the LORD require of you? To act justly and to love mercy and to walk humbly with your God. (Micah 6:8)

17

JESUS PREACHED UNITY

Jesus calls us to unity in him. He prayed for his followers to be one, just as he and the Father are one. This unity is not based on political affiliation but on our shared commitment to follow Christ and his teachings. It is our common faith in Jesus that should bind us together, transcending our political differences.

> That they all may be one, as You, Father, are in Me, and I in You; that they also may be one in Us, that the world may believe that You sent Me. (John 17:21 NKJV)

> Behold, how good and how pleasant it is
> For brethren to dwell together in unity!
> (Psalm 133:1 NKJV)

CONCLUSION

As we navigate the complex intersection of faith and politics, it is crucial for you to remember that Jesus is neither Republican nor Democrat. He is something far better than our frail human political parties could ever offer. His teachings always challenge us to rise above all political divisions and embrace a Christ-centered perspective. Let us prioritize love, compassion, justice, and the kingdom of God in our political engagement, always striving to reflect the character of Jesus in our actions and decisions.

Let us commit to always be on Jesus' side.

DISCUSSION & REFLECTION

1. How does the intersection of faith and politics challenge Christians to navigate their values and convictions?

2. In what ways can Christians actively engage in the political process while still prioritizing the teachings and example of Jesus?

3. Why is it important for Christians to approach partisan politics with discernment and humility, seeking common ground and the common good?

COME LET US REASON TOGETHER

JUSTIN VALENTINE

Senior Pastor of Kingdom Life Church

BELIEVE IT OR NOT, I love politics—I enjoy the numbers, the polling, and even the campaign. It gives me the same feeling as watching a good boxing match or football game. There was a time when every TV in my house had a different news channel on. I could even watch C-SPAN!

I don't know about you, but it seems that as I get older, every election cycle becomes even more polarizing and divisive than the one before it. Perhaps it has always been this way, and I just didn't know it. Or have things gotten a little more tense in our lifetimes?

We often hear politically minded folks say, "This could be the most important election in our lifetime." For those who are fully engaged in an "all or nothing" posture, this can become

a self-fulfilling prophecy. Each side gravitates toward their re-
spective corners with childlike faith, ready to fight until they get
their way, and fully believing that the prosperity of the nation is
riding on the outcome of the election.

Even more shocking than the polarization of secular political subsets is what happens to us Christians during these election cycles. I once heard a preacher say, and I could relate, that
if he could put all his friends in a single room, they would probably end up killing each other because of how deeply they held
their *political* convictions!

How did we get here? Aren't we the redeemed body of
Christ? We are those who have been called to a mission to reach
the lost with the love of Jesus. Well . . . that is until our four-year
rinse-and-repeat political cycle starts. Unfortunately, it seems
that many of us lose the true mission of Jesus in all the noise
and bluster of partisan politics.

The prophet Isaiah lived in a time of great political tension
and upheaval in ancient Israel. Though his words are far older
than America, you and I can still glean from his wisdom today.
If we would learn from these words, I believe Isaiah's wisdom
would greatly help us in our own discourse and discussions.
In the beginning of Isaiah 1:18 NKJV, the prophet, speaking the
words of God to Israel, proclaims, "Come now, and let us reason
together."

What does it mean to *reason*? In my understanding, rea-
soning is how one arrives at a conclusion; it's how we make up
our minds. Have you heard the adage, so-and-so "just won't listen to reason"? By this, we're insinuating that a person will not
heed practical wisdom. Or we are implying that the person has
made up their mind in a foolish way.

But everyone has reason, or "a reason." As we enter this new
political season, I would encourage us all to keep this in mind.

We are all an amalgamation of our personal experiences, history, and upbringing. These factors combine and coalesce, leading us each to reason and draw conclusions in unique ways.

Now, we may not like someone's reason, but have we taken the time to fully understand how someone arrived at their personal conclusions? Have we slowed down enough to examine our own viewpoints through another person's lens? Have we been meek enough to stand in someone else's shoes and see the world through their eyes?

We are so often tempted to get frustrated with our neighbors and the folks in our broader community. I think much of the angst we experience comes from feeling like we haven't been heard or listened to well. But have we offered this type of deep understanding to others—the very listening that we ourselves have desired to receive? Perhaps the frustration we sense in others emerges from a similar feeling of not being heard.

What should our goal and mission as followers of Jesus be when coming into another election season? Our ultimate mission can't just be to get everyone to agree with our own political perspective. Isn't the mission of the church something that transcends seasonal, human politics?

Let's return to our key text in Isaiah. This passage has something profound to speak to us about the deeper mission for Christians. The prophet Isaiah said,

> "Come now, and let us reason together,"
> Says the LORD,
> 'Though your sins are like scarlet,
> They shall be white as snow;
> Though they are red like crimson,
> They shall be as wool."

Here we find truth that transcends all the earthly political arguments, debates, parties, and structures that we will encounter this year. The common ground is that God desires to have a relationship with us, but we *all* have an issue with sin. All have sinned and fallen short of God's glory. Our sin is like scarlet but, through the work of Christ, God desires to make us "white as snow." Everyone shares this common problem; our sin is a crimson stain that can only be remedied by the precious blood of Jesus.

Among Christians, the heart of Christ should be increasingly on display, especially in divisive times. Our mission as followers of Jesus is to proclaim to our brothers and sisters the work of the cross. The cross reconciles us to God and teaches us to walk in the ministry of reconciliation toward one another.

My admonishment to fellow Christians during this season is to maintain our heads, to retain our focus, and to remember the mission. Our mission is always pointing people to Jesus. May we be a people who like Paul can "become all things to all people," (1 Corinthians 9:22) so that we might win a few.

Everyone has "a reason," and everyone has rationale for their reason. But we should also remember that reason doesn't necessarily come from pure rationality. Because we are a combination of our experiences, everyone arrives at their beliefs through a unique journey. I might not like your reason (you may not like mine), and I might not fully understand your rationale, but we must respect one another enough to listen to one another and maintain our care for one another.

When we learn to reason together, and as Christians keep the main mission in mind, we can see the election cycle as an opportunity. This season provides us a unique chance to get to know our neighbors, friends, and family members through careful listening. Perhaps we will even get to know and understand our neighbors and family members in a deeper way as we take the time to humbly listen to their perspectives and con-

COME LET US REASON TOGETHER

cerns. Through good listening we can get an understanding of their needs. What are they looking for? What are they worried about? What are their fears?

In most cases, when we dig into this, we can find common ground with anyone. Don't you believe that your unsaved friends love their children too? Don't you think that your Muslim friends want an opportunity for their sons and daughters to flourish and prosper as well? Even an atheist would like to drink clean water and live in peace. Don't you desire these same things?

If we are willing to look for shared values, we will likely find much common ground on political issues. We would miss these shared concerns if we aren't patient enough to look and listen.

That doesn't mean as Christians we don't have non-negotiables. Christians have always believed that there is truth worth suffering for, and in extreme cases, even dying for. For everyone reading this article, it is almost certainly true that you have room to grow in your listening skills (as do I). The purpose of this article is to help realign our souls with the heart of Jesus, *not* to reason away our faith. So learning to listen well to others is key in our discipleship process, but we also stand on the truth of Christ.

This political season is also an opportunity to share our message of hope. Don't we believe that Christ also cares about the same things we care about (our children flourishing, our businesses thriving, the hungry fed, etc.)? The hot-button topics of the day may divide us, but there is humanity in all of us. Christians believe that every single man, woman, and child is created in God's image. We all long for love, acceptance, and community. These are all traits we find in Christ and can find in each other if we'll listen well.

What if we listened to one another well enough to acquire a true understanding of reason? Jesus was an incredible listener. If we learned to listen like he listened, we would have so many chances to share his love with those we are listening to. Paul became all things to all people so he could win some. As we listen, converse, and reason with one another, the Holy Spirit can plant seeds through our conversations. The work of the Holy Spirit in someone's life may be the way that someone comes into relationship with Jesus.

In Isaiah 1:17, the Lord says, "Learn to do right; seek justice. Defend the oppressed. Take up the cause of the fatherless; plead the case of the widow." Can you imagine a world where this was true? These beautiful statements are all part of God's mission to save the world through the work of Christ. Whether or not they are Christian, most people desire these things to be true too. We're all attempting to address our concerns and fears from slightly different angles and viewpoints. Let's be a people who reason well, and who give other people a chance to share their reasons too.

DISCUSSION & REFLECTION

1. What would it look like for you to intentionally take time to listen well to a neighbor, coworker, or family member you've been avoiding?

2. How do you feel about God saying to humans, "Come now, and let us reason together"? How would you respond to God if he said that to you?

BETTER TOGETHER

JOSH PARK

A Founding Pastor of Branch Life Church

IN THE MID 1990s my high school basketball team, the Eagles, was steeped in an intense rivalry with the Cougars. Like any good Philadelphia-area athlete, we took our rivalries seriously. We considered the Cougars an enemy deserving complete and utter disdain. Each year in the weeks leading up to the big game our coach would review the key players by name, and we'd set up our battle plan to crush them. I'm sure they did the same.

I'm also certain my name did not come up in their preparation. I wasn't much of an athletic threat but more of a uniformed statistician. I still played my part of loyal team member, knowing well the names, jersey numbers and faces of each enemy Cougar. When game day arrived, the Cougars sat on their side of the bleachers as we sat on our side mocking each other and preparing for war.

To be clear, we were not friends on or off the field. It was *us versus them*.

Fast-forward twenty-five years. I'm no longer a high school bench warmer, passionate about winning a championship banner to hang in perpetuity in the high school gymnasium with our season's years displayed for all to see. I'm now a happily married, sleep-deprived father of two, with multiple degrees, twenty years of pastoral experience, a golden retriever, and blue pick-up truck. The names, jersey numbers, and faces of our high school rivals have been lost to time and an over-caffeinated brain.

In 2018 we moved to the Pottstown area, which just happens to be halfway between my old high school and our rivals, the Cougars.

I've also learned to focus less on rivalry and more on community. What if instead of *us versus them* it was **us and them?** Through a series of life-altering crises God has taught me the power of community, the blessing of unity, and the importance of togetherness. The wisest man to ever live puts it this way in Ecclesiastes 4:9, "Two are better than one."

Today, as I'm sure you are aware, we live in a world divided. It is a world of *us versus them*. Each election year the division seems to grow wider and wider. Division isn't a new problem; it is a problem as old as the garden of Eden, when mankind divided from God because of sin. Ever since Adam and Eve ate the forbidden fruit, everything God has done has been to bring us back together. The tragic effect of sin is that division has marked every culture throughout human history including our own. America did come together to fight for our independence, but at the same time we formed separate states. After the 9/11 attacks, all of Congress gathered on the steps of the Capitol, unified as Americans singing the national anthem. But by the next election cycle the partisan divide reemerged.

During the State of Union, Republicans sit on their side of the room and the Democrats on the other, mocking each other, and preparing for war. *It is, after all, us versus them.*

What divides us is not just politics but also race, religion, education, socio-economic policies, immigration, and so on. These issues mark us and move us into camps, tribes, parties, and even into a civil war. Unity, it seems, has never been our thing. It appears that the American way has always been *us versus them.*

That's what makes the Bible's teaching about unity so radical. God says in John 13:35 that true Christ followers will be known by their love, by their ... *unity.* In a divided world, Christians who love one another and love their neighbor the way God intended will stick out like a ruby rose in a garden of white.

John 15:5 gives us a powerful picture of the power of unity. Jesus says, "I am the vine; you are the branches. If you remain in me and I in you, you will bear much fruit; apart from me you can do nothing."

A branch is only as strong as its connection to the tree (unity). Only together with the tree does the branch bear fruit. By working together, the branches of the tree give shade, substance, and shelter to its neighbors. Every one of every race, every age, every gender, every religion, and every political party will be blessed by the branches of those who abide in Christ.

Us versus them is not what Jesus teaches. Jesus teaches **we are better together.**

We are *better together* with Christ.

We are *better together* with our local church family.

We are *better together* with our wider Christian community.

We are *better together* with our neighbors.

We are *better together* with our community.

This election year you will hear many, many voices preaching the message of rivalry and division. It will be proclaimed by politicians and pundits, celebrities and musicians, and by neighbors and strangers. It will be on your feeds, your phones, televisions, podcasts, newspapers, and blogs. The message of Jesus must be louder. It must be declared and demonstrated. The message of Jesus is a message of *unity*. The message the church is called to proclaim is that *we are better together*.

Yes, you'll be asked to cast your vote (which you should prayerfully and thoughtfully do), but always remember your politics should never become your primary identity, your salvation, or your hope. Remember too that people who vote differently are not your rivals, they are your neighbors.

As Christians, our identity is in Christ, our salvation comes from the King of Kings, not the president the United States. And our hope comes from God's Word. As the church, our mission is not *us versus them* but it is **us for them.**

"For God so loved the world that he gave . . . ." John 3:16 says that God is so for them that he gave his one and only Son so that the world might be saved. That is the radical kind of love Christian voters must be known for.

During my time in the Pottstown area, our mission has been to live out the truth that we are better together. Our church works hard to strengthen our connection to Christ, to love each other, to bless other churches, and to give generously to our community.

When a fire destroyed an area apartment building in 2020, our community came together to feed, fund, clothe, and re-house over fifty families. Over one hundred thousand dollars, mountains of physical donations, and hundreds of gift cards came from all over our community, and over a dozen different churches worked together to walk with these families from crisis to recovery. *We are better together.*

When Hurricane Ida caused county-wide flooding in 2021, the county partnered with over twenty-five churches to re-house 150 families. *We are better together.*

When an explosion rocked a Pottstown neighborhood in 2022, displacing ten families, our faith community banded together to mourn, give, and begin the process of rebuilding. *We are better together.*

Through crises big and small we have seen time and again why Jesus teaches us that we truly are better together. Three key reasons demonstrate this:

- Together with community partners and kingdom partners we can do far more than we could ever do alone. One leaf doesn't offer much shade, but a tree full of them does!
- The world is full of people who aren't looking a for worship service but who are looking for acts of service. When they know that you care, then they care about what you know.
- Partnerships with other community leaders, pastors, ministry leaders, nonprofits, politicians, and local officials can turn into beautiful friendships leading to opportunities to love and be loved by people of every tribe.

We are better together!

One community partner we've served beside these past few years is a man named Tim. Tim has become like family even though we don't attend the same church or even hold all the same theological views (who does?). Tim has been an amazing partner in community life, in ministry, and in crisis response. He has been a shoulder to cry on, a friend to pray with, and a leader to serve alongside. In a twist of fate only God could arrange, Tim was number 21 on the Cougars' basketball team. In high school he was one of those enemy basketball players our coached warned us about in those pre-game huddles. He was *them*. Little did I know that someone who was once an enemy would one day become a lifelong friend.

In this election year let's preach the radical message of unity, let's learn how to work together even when we disagree, and let's be known by our love. Blessed are the peacemakers, because Jesus is the Savior of the world and because *we are better together*.

DISCUSSION & REFLECTION

1. In what ways have you seen politics divide Christians from the world and from one another?

2. What does it mean to *fight for unity*? (see Ephesians 4:1–6)

3. How do the following examples from Jesus demonstrate we are better together?

   - Matthew the tax collector becoming one of the twelve apostles.
   - Jesus eating at Zacchaeus the tax collector's house
   - The message of salvation being given to Jews and Gentiles
   - The story of the Good Samaritan

4. In a divided world what are some practical ways Christians can become known for our love for others, not division? (online, in our neighborhoods, and in our homes, etc.)

ONE THING

JOE TERRERI

Lead Pastor of Connection Church

> Anything without a head is dead. Anything with
> more than one head is a monster. Jesus Christ is
> the only true head of the church.
>
> —H.B. Charles Jr.[1]

IF YOU EVER WANT TO find out how patient you are, coach Little League baseball. When my son Joseph started playing Tee Ball, the team already had a coach. I wanted to be involved as much as I could be, so I offered to be the assistant. It's impossible to have too much help at a Tee Ball game! Most kids don't know what direction to run after they hit the ball or what base to throw to if the ball is hit to them.

That first season didn't go that great. Our coach wasn't very engaged and didn't even show up for the last game of the season.

I ended up coaching in his place. During that year I discovered I enjoyed working with kids. I especially liked the ability to make sure my own son was having a good time. That last game of Tee Ball was the day I decided I would volunteer to coach going forward.

Over the next four seasons, I got to coach my son and the same core group of kids. We went to four championship games and won three of them. Now, this is an important moment to disclose that the league only had four teams, so please feel free to remain unimpressed. I'd love to say, "It was all coaching." But we had some of the best players in the league and good odds. I need to disclose something else: I loved winning. I'm competitive by nature. Don't tell anyone, but I was taking Little League baseball a bit too seriously.

It still bothers me that we lost one of the championship games. I have a second-place medal lying around somewhere at home collecting dust. Celebrating a second-place finish always feels silly to me. "You almost did it . . . but not quite." I tend to agree with the adage that second place is first loser. I don't think there is a Christian around who wants Jesus to be in second place.

When the apostle Paul writes to the Colossians, he wants them to know the glory, grandeur, and greatness of Jesus Christ. This young church was being influenced by false teachers who were asserting that Jesus Christ wasn't enough. It's not that the false teachers thought Jesus didn't matter, it's that they were saying he wasn't sufficient. Paul's primary strategy to combat this poisonous teaching was to exalt Jesus Christ and show the church just how awesome he is.

Colossians 1:15–20 is widely believed to be some kind of early church hymn or creedal confession. It's possible that Paul wrote it himself or adapted it for the church. However, these verses contain some of the richest theological truths about Jesus in the New Testament. It's possible to write a whole book just on this passage. But for our purposes I want us to think about verses 17–18.

> He is before all things, and in him all things hold together. And he is the head of the body, the church; he is the beginning and the firstborn from among the dead, so that in everything he might have the supremacy.

Let's take a moment to briefly reflect on these truths.

Jesus is before all things, meaning that there is no one or no thing that matters more than he does.

Jesus is holding all things together. The very existence of the universe and our very existence are totally dependent on him. Or to put that another way, if Jesus were to somehow choose to stop holding all things together, everything would immediately disintegrate.

Jesus is the head of his body, the church. In this context, the word *head* means the person who is in charge. The church is the body of Jesus, but he is in charge of his body.

Jesus is the firstborn from among the dead. Paul is not saying that Jesus is a created being. The meaning of *firstborn* is that Jesus preceded all others in something very specific: his resurrection. Jesus was the first to rise from the grave, and the hope of the Christian is that we will one day rise like he rose (1 Corinthians 15:20–23).

But notice that Paul doesn't leave these spectacular realities in a vacuum. He says that because all of this is true, **Jesus must have the supremacy in everything.** Jesus Christ is in first place. The one who holds all things together will never accept a second-place medal. He is supreme over everyone and everything.

There can only be one thing or one person who occupies the place of supremacy. It's illogical for those of us who are married to say, *"My spouse is supremely important to me and my job is supremely important to me."* Supremacy can only apply to a single entity (by its very definition). It's impossible for both things to be true.

Our churches can easily push Jesus out of the seat of supremacy without even realizing it. Instead of our life together as the people of God being centered on Christ, we can become centered on our preferences, our dress code, our activism, our convenience, our social standing, or even our pastors. I'm sure it wouldn't take long for you to think of your own examples of how churches displace the supremacy of Christ in everything.

A real obvious and tragic arena for us to make church life about something other than Christ is in our politics. When partisan politics becomes a central aspect of our churches, we cease to be the church. In fact, we become a different entity all together. When churches galvanize around a party or candidate and then attach Jesus' name to it, we turn our Savior into our mascot.

The moment Jesus Christ ceases to have the place of supremacy in our churches is the moment we cease to be the church.

Take a moment to consider the storyline of the book of Acts. After Jesus ascends into heaven, he sends his Spirit to empower his followers to be his witnesses (Acts 1:8). Immediately, the early church goes from a group of 120 in Jerusalem to several thousand scattered throughout Judea, Samaria, and to the outer reaches of the Roman Empire. Every time I read through Acts, I am astonished by the Spirit moving through ordinary people to continue Jesus' work. However, there is not a single instance where the first followers of Jesus consumed themselves with political activism.

I want to challenge you to read through the sermons in the book of Acts. As you read them, you'll discover that none of them were political in nature. In fact, all of them were about one Person and his supremacy over not only Israel but also over the whole world. At no point did the early church concern itself with taking down Rome, fighting for their rights, or grasping for power. The early church was consumed with Jesus and spreading the gospel to the ends of the earth. The early church was consumed with Jesus' mission.

My point is not that it's wrong for God's people to be politically engaged. My point is that if we aren't diligent, we can allow our personal political beliefs and convictions to distract us from Jesus' mission. Jesus didn't come to seek and save a voting bloc. Jesus came to seek and save the lost (Luke 19:10). Jesus called us into making disciples of all nations and teaching them to obey everything he commanded (Matthew 28:18–20). When our pulpits and small groups and Sunday school classes slowly turn into a place for political talking points instead of proclaiming Christ, Jesus isn't having the supremacy, and we aren't being the church.

When the church gets political in a partisan manner it always gets divided. If our churches are tacitly implying that serious Christians are all on one side of the aisle, then our unity isn't based on our common experience of being reconciled to God through faith in Jesus Christ, our unity is based on donkeys and elephants. It's fine to have strong political convictions and to vote your conscience, but that's not the mission.

Many bemoan the weakness and ineffectiveness of the American church and point the finger at a secular culture. I too am saddened by our collective slide into godlessness. However,

I wonder what it would be like if the American church looked in the mirror and asked if Jesus Christ has the supremacy in every detail of our churches, families, and hearts? Let's recommit ourselves to being about his business in the world and refuse to accept a counterfeit mission. Let's never allow Jesus to be in second place.

DISCUSSION & REFLECTION

1. Read Colossians 1:15–20. What stands out to you?

2. How have you seen or experienced Jesus not having supremacy in the local church?

3. What can you do personally to ensure that Jesus has the supremacy in your own life?

4. What can you do to help your church family keep Jesus at the center of church life?

WATCH AND PRAY

TIM DOERING

Founder of Netzer

Jesus said, "My kingdom is not of this world. If it were, my servants would fight to prevent my arrest by the Jewish leaders. But now my kingdom is from another place."

—John 18:36

ONE OF THE SCENES IN the gospel narrative that most broadens my imagination takes place in the garden of Gethsemane. Jesus has just fought perhaps the biggest battle of his life, a cosmic war waged in prayer. His closest friends and followers slept through the battle. Are we meant to feel the painful irony?

We may be reminded of another story that took place not too long before this one, in which Jesus was the one sleeping

45

while they were in a state of panic. They had been facing the raging seas, struggling to maintain control of their boat during a violent storm. When they woke Jesus, he rebuked them for their lack of faith.

Is it that same lack of trust that allows them to now sleep in the garden while Jesus faces the most significant storm of all? Even his clear words didn't keep them awake: "Watch and pray so that you will not fall into temptation. The spirit is willing, but the flesh is weak" (Matthew 26:41). Maybe if they had understood what was really happening that night, they would have found themselves more capable. This is the tricky thing about faith, though, isn't it? Faith calls us to believe that what the Lord says is real, is what is true. Our instincts, however, tell us that reality is discovered through our senses, experiences, and logical deduction.

His friends' faith, often like mine, was too small. As a result, Jesus fought alone. Yet, Jesus fought to win—by being willing to lose. This is hard to wrap our heads around. Jesus was fully prayed up. He was prepared to not reciprocate the injustice and violence coming his way. The things Jesus was about to endure were horrific. How he would handle them was decided in his time of prayer. The trauma that one of his friends, Peter, would face that evening was also intensely disturbing. Was Peter's own violent reaction and then denial of Jesus also determined in the garden by his lack of prayer?

Jesus emerges from his epic spiritual struggle resolute. The subsequent encounter in John 18 reveals the fruit of our Lord's prayerful clarity. Judas came to the garden with the chief priest's soldiers. Knowing their intentions, Jesus asked who they were looking for. When they said they were looking for "Jesus of Nazareth," Jesus faced a clear choice. Acknowledging his identity meant embracing a brutal, torturous death. But the choice was already made as he knelt before his Father in prayer. So, he yields to reality and walks directly into the coming torrent. "I am he."

We are told that when he said, "I am he," the soldiers fell backward! Here, my imagination is pressed. What was that scene like? How did that happen? What a profound moment! Is this a preview of the deepest reality? We know that one day in the future, every knee will bow before Jesus, and every tongue will confess that he is Lord. At this moment, he is the one who confesses who he is. And as he steps into that reality, with all its pain, his kingdom comes on earth in a way that puts his assailants down on their backsides. Suddenly, their clubs and swords seem frightfully unimpressive.

This scene is a peek beyond the physical veil as the spiritual power of Christ's majesty manifests in the physical realm. The stage is set. It is now evident that Jesus is the one holding the other-worldly power. He will engage the coming hours, the hateful religious leaders, and self-seeking politicians with enormous authority, but he will never use it to seek control of others. He will, instead, choose to use his power to remain in control of *himself* by trusting his Father. He will bring faith, hope, and even love into the dark recesses of the devil's lair, exposing how empty of power the prince of darkness' throne is.

Through the sequence of events that follow, various leaders jockey for strategic advantages that they believe will allow them to maintain their small measure of control over their temporary positions of power. On that day, when the King of Kings came to town, they chose not to see reality. They continued using the worldly power structures they knew to leverage their own agendas. Jesus had proven to be a formidable disruptor of the system. Their systems were built on false assurances and unrealities. When they bumped up against the One who was the Truth, it exposed just how fragile their domain actually was. It became clear that their kingdoms would eventually crumble. But those systems were their means of maintaining power. Christ, refusing to fear their authority, needed to be eliminated. For Jesus, the next twenty-four hours were the test of his meekness, his restraint, his faith in his Father, and his love for his people.

It was not only people and politicians that wanted to get rid of him. The demons and the devil himself were even more fully aware of the threat that Jesus posed to their domain. Jesus knew that the ultimate battle would not be fought against the religious leaders, Pilate, or Caesar. The mentality that shaped the Roman Empire and the false narratives that formed thrones for the devil in the hearts of humans needed to be confronted. If Christ's people would be free, it would be by revealing a greater power. He would not need to flex external force. Rather, he would embrace internal faith, restraint, and fortitude. He would receive the worst of what those systems threatened for those who did not submit to them. And he would, by faith, spiritually overcome them, living according to the reality of his heavenly kingdom.

This whole passion story is the victory and inauguration of King Jesus. What does it now look like for us to seek his reign among us? Undoubtedly, it means that we must not yield to the false reality of power and systems rooted in human authority. We will not look to kings and rulers as our hope. Instead, we will look to Christ. Voting is one of the incredible privileges of living in a democracy. But prayer is infinitely more powerful and is a far more tremendous honor for the children of the King. Voting and prayer are not mutually exclusive, but they are nowhere close to being equal.

Friend, will you, through faith, embrace reality? Will you believe that the power of heaven is more significant than any earthly throne? Will you embrace your own identity and calling as a child and priest of God? Will you use your access to the throne room of the King of Kings to pray for his kingdom to come and his will to be done here on earth this election year? Will you choose to set aside what may be in your personal best interest in the outcome of the election? Will you seek first the kingdom of God and his righteousness? If so, then I urge you to avoid the cultural wars rooted in polarizing politics. Instead, I encourage you to engage in the more profound battle for the things that Christ prayed for in John 17 as he walked to the garden. Pray that we, his people, would be *one*, that his kingdom would come, and his will would be done, among us.

DISCUSSION & REFLECTION

> I urge, then, first of all, that petitions, prayers, intercession and thanksgiving be made for all people—for kings and all those in authority, that we may live peaceful and quiet lives in all godliness and holiness. (1 Timothy 2:1–2)

1. Do you find the directions of this verse easy or challenging to agree with?

2. Do you find the instructions of this verse difficult to practice?

3. How do you imagine it would look to implement this verse in your life more fully?

4. What would someone need to believe to feel compelled to live out this verse more completely?

> This, then, is how you should pray: "Our Father in heaven, hallowed be your name, your kingdom come, your will be done, on earth as it is in heaven." (Matthew 6:9–10)

5. Notice that the prayer for the coming of Christ's kingdom follows the praise of the Father. How could consistent prayers of exaltation of God affect the minds of Christians in an election year?

6. What do we do when different principles of Christ's kingdom seem to be championed by competing political parties?

7. What prayers could be prayed in agreement between God's people, even when they disagree about who should hold a political office?

8. What prayers are you willing to contend for in response to these verses?

RESILIENT DISCIPLESHIP: A GENERATION PREPARED FOR BABYLON

BRANDON BEST
Area Director for Young Life Tri-County

I F YOU ARE A HISTORY buff like me, then perhaps you'll understand why war movies and shows are one of my favorite genres. *Saving Private Ryan, Band of Brothers,* and *The Pacific* are a few of my favorites about WWII. When I was sixteen, I had the opportunity to visit Normandy with my family. I was in awe and felt like I was walking on holy ground. Unlike the Jersey Shore, the beaches of Normandy are made up of cliffs and bluffs. I still wonder, *How in the world did the Allied forces defeat the Nazis? The Nazis clearly had every tactical advantage.* It seems like all those obstacles would have made it an impossible mission.

Today's task of reaching younger generations with the gospel may seem equally impregnable. The cliffs may appear unassailable. Currently, about sixty-four percent of teenagers leave the church by the age of thirty.

Some commentators have pointed out that living as a Christian in today's environment is like living as exiles in Babylon. How should the church respond to this difficult task of raising children in the faith at such a difficult moment? As a parent, I understand the urge to shelter my children from the brokenness of the world. I want to protect my children. I don't want them to be primarily influenced by the things of this world. This is a natural response. Many of the parents I talk to in various churches and denominations throughout Pottstown feel the same way.

Our desire to shelter our children can come with several unique challenges. One problem is that we will never be able to completely shelter our children from everything. A second potential issue is that of overprotection. Our kids need to face difficult situations and challenges to grow the resiliency necessary for them to become faithful, godly adults navigating a broken world.

The Scriptures reveal the importance of *resilient discipleship*. A resilient disciple is someone who wants to be with Jesus, to become like Jesus, and to learn to live the way he does in the face of opposition. Some of my favorite biblical examples of resilient disciples are the early church in Acts, as well as Daniel, Nehemiah, and Ezra during the exilic period.

Resilient discipleship speaks into our cultural moment because we are often discipled more by the political ideologies of our day than by the God of the universe. The only way we can withstand the trials, suffering, division, and unbiblical political ideologies is through resilient discipleship.

In this article, I want to highlight the story of King Josiah. Josiah was himself a resilient disciple whom God used to raise up a generation of faithful disciples able to navigate the complexities of life in pagan Babylon.

When we read 1 and 2 Kings and 1 and 2 Chronicles, we see how king after king did evil. Time and again, Scripture says, "And he did what was evil in the sight of the Lord." King Josiah was the sixteenth king of Judah and reigned from about 640 to 609 BC. Second Chronicles 34:2 describes Josiah as a man who "did what was right in the eyes of the LORD, and followed the ways of his father David, not turning aside to the right or to the left." Josiah had a deep relationship with God, one that had not been seen in a leader in Israel since King David. Israelites who would end up in Babylon witnessed in Josiah an example worth following. Until about ten years old, Daniel, Meshach, Shadrach, and Abednego witnessed the leadership of Josiah.

To cultivate a resilient discipleship in our children, they need examples of resilient discipleship that they can witness firsthand. Paul says, "Follow my example, as I follow the example of Christ" (1 Corinthians 11:1). Similarly, I believe that the example of Josiah can help us build resilient disciples in today's context.

JOSIAH OBEYED GOD'S COMMANDS

Josiah celebrated the Passover for the first time in generations. It may have been the greatest celebration of the Passover since Exodus 12. Second Chronicles 35:18 says, "The Passover had not been observed like this in Israel since the days of the prophet Samuel; and none of the kings of Israel had ever celebrated such a Passover as did Josiah." This must have been an incredible festival to observe and one of the biggest celebrations in Israelite history.

I have FOMO about this celebration! The Passover festival was a signpost pointing to the death and resurrection of Jesus. It symbolized how God would ultimately deliver us from the bondage of slavery to sin through Jesus. To disciple our own children well, we must celebrate the death and resurrection of Jesus like Josiah celebrated that Passover. The death and resurrection of Jesus are the crucial ingredients in building resilient disciples. Our children must see how Jesus' death and resurrection are central to our lives. If our children do not have this as the key part of being a resilient disciple, nothing else will matter. Without this, we're likely talking about behavior modification, not discipleship. Jesus, the true Passover Lamb, is the greatest example of resilient discipleship.

JOSIAH WAS COMMITTED
TO THE SCRIPTURES

Josiah also had a profound commitment to Scripture that led to great steps of faith. In 2 Chronicles 34, as Israel worked on the temple, purging it of idols, they rediscovered the Hebrew Scriptures. When the scroll was read to Josiah, he tore his clothes (2 Chronicles 34:19). His actions showed his grief and repentance. Josiah then renewed his commitment to God in view of all the Israelites. The Israelites themselves then renewed their own commitment to follow the commands of God.

We see this renewed commitment to God play out beautifully in the book of Daniel. In this exilic book, resilient discipleship is exemplified by Daniel's refusal to eat the king's food and break kosher laws (Daniel 1:8). We also witness resilient discipleship through the Israelite boys' rejection of other gods, refusing to bow to the golden statue (Daniel 3). Additionally, we observe Daniel's profound commitment to God in the story of his praying only to the true God, and as a result facing down the danger of the lions' den (Daniel 6).

Like young Daniel, it's vitally important for our children to know Scripture. The messages of Babylon tell our children that their identity and value come from things other than Christ. But everything this world offers is rubbish. The Scriptures reveal that our true value and identity come from Christ alone.

One of the best examples of this is in the baptism of Jesus. The Father said of Jesus, "This is my Son, whom I love; with him I am well pleased" (Matthew 3:17). From there Jesus went into the wilderness to face down the lies of Satan. Jesus journeyed confidently into the wasteland because he knew who he belonged to, he knew his identity as God's Son, and he knew that the Father was already pleased with him.

In our context, for the emerging generation to go confidently into the wilderness they must know the same things. A disciple's identity is that of a son or daughter of the Most-High God. They are deeply loved and belong to God. A disciple's mission and purpose is to be a faithful servant of God. And, even when they feel like a failure, God still loves them fully because they are his in Christ.

JOSIAH REJECTED IDOLS

King Josiah also destroyed the idols throughout all of Judah. In 2 Chronicles 34:3–7, Josiah tore down altars, smashed the idols, and took all the broken pieces and scattered them among the graves of the people who worshiped idols. This may come off as a bit intense! But it shows that Josiah was serious about getting rid of the idols that distracted Israel from worshiping the true God.

We see a similar commitment in the next generation through the stories of Shadrach, Meshach, and Abednego.

Think about their refusal to bend down to Nebuchadnezzar and worship him. They stand as a beautiful example of what Paul wrote to the Roman church, "Do not conform to the pattern of this world, but be transformed by the renewing of your mind. Then you will be able to test and approve what God's will is—his good, pleasing and perfect will" (Romans 12:2). Too many times we come across as more of a disciple of the Republican or Democratic party rather than being a disciple of Jesus. Resilient discipleship allows us to withstand the things of this world and allows us to be transformed by the God of the universe.

As we seek to raise up the next generation of resilient disciples, we do not need to be frozen by fear. Just like King Josiah and the generation of exiles that grew up during his reign, our situation should bring us to our knees in prayer. Paul wrote to a group of believers seeking to be resilient disciples amid the Roman Empire, "Do not be anxious about anything, but in every situation, by prayer and petition, with thanksgiving, present your requests to God. And the peace of God, which transcends all understanding, will guard your hearts and your minds in Christ Jesus" (Philippians 4:6–7). May we make our requests known to God, may our children be faithful servants even within the empires of this world, and may the peace of God give us the understanding and courage to help us to build up a generation of resilient disciples.

DISCUSSION & REFLECTION

1. Look at how you have voted over the past and where you get your news from. What political ideologies do you allow to speak into your life over Jesus?

2. Can you, like Josiah, identify idols in your life? How might you go about removing these idols from your life?

3. What spiritual disciplines do you regularly practice? How often do you do them? Can these spiritual disciplines begin to shape your heart and mind in Christ in new ways?

WHAT YOUR BODY IS SAYING ABOUT THIS ELECTION

CHRIS McCARTY

Deacon at Parker Ford Church & a family Physician

> Do not be afraid of those who kill the body but cannot kill the soul. Rather, be afraid of the One who can destroy both soul and body . . . .
>
> —Matthew 10:28

EVERYONE IS TALKING ABOUT THIS election. How could you not? A presidential rematch? Global conflicts? Economic instability? I see why people say, "This is the most important election ever!" (Fun fact. That phrase was first used in newspaper ads for a governor's race in 1805 and now gets used for every election.)

There is someone else who wants to chime in about this election: your body. And you really should listen to what it's trying to say.

Political stress affects everyone. It's important to realize the impact that the constant stream of divisive arguments has on your emotional and physical health. If we properly listen to those "gut feelings," we can identify early warning signs that the stress and pressure are too much. Let's learn how to hear what our body has to say and some steps we can take to protect ourselves.

THE RISE OF ANXIETY AND DEPRESSION

The rates of both anxiety and its ugly cousin, depression, have been increasing over the past few decades. According to a Gallup poll, nearly four out of ten adults worldwide report being affected by these mental illnesses.[1]

It's narrow-minded to blame this increase solely on political factors such as the rise of partisan polarization and the round-the-clock political news cycle. But let's just say those two factors haven't helped.

The only thing growing faster than our country's political polarization is our perception of it. Research shows that Americans consistently overestimate polarization.[2] That means you probably think people who vote differently than you have more radical views than they do in reality.

This encourages us to create a paradigm of "good" versus "evil," where we are fighting to protect the country's future. And this has significant effects on our emotional health. Americans with higher levels of perceived political polarization are significantly more likely to develop anxiety and depression.[3]

There also is reason to point fingers at certain factions of the media. The twenty-four-hour news cycle thrives on ratings.

To keep you tuning in, some news organizations play off your emotions. This is why they sensationalize stories, stirring up fear, anger, and indignation. It's also why the next election is always the most important ever. This gets compounded by hearing the stories over and over. It is not uncommon to hear about the same issue from multiple media personalities in one evening, each one trying harder than the first to kindle strong emotions. These emotions initially make you feel motivated and inspired, but they are taking a toll on your health. As you would expect, people who consume more critical political media coverage report worse psychological and physical health.[4]

LISTENING TO YOUR BODY

I'm a family physician, which means that I am constantly trying to decipher what people's bodies are telling them. Yes, I can order tests, but I first listen carefully to signs and symptoms (the body's language).

Did you know family doctors spend more time and energy dealing with anxiety and depression than any other medical problem? Just diagnosing them can be challenging. It's rare that someone comes to my office believing that they are suffering from these mental illnesses. Instead, they have constellations of physical symptoms that point toward mental health concerns.

You can learn your body's language and better understand the impact of political stress. Below are some of the classic ways our bodies tell us the stress is too much:

- **Feeling tired.** Your "get up and go" got up and went. You may also notice that you stop doing things you typically enjoy, such as walking your dog or

63

getting together with friends (especially those who have differing belief systems).

- **Problems sleeping.** This can be either too much or too little sleep. Your sleep habits may have suddenly changed and you feel like you just always need more sleep, but you can't get it when you try.
- **Headaches.** Frequent frustrating headaches are common. If you have migraines, you may notice them getting worse.
- **Dizziness.** Many people complain of a lightheaded feeling or being off balance.
- **Tingling sensations.** This is most likely in your hands or lips but could be anywhere.
- **Chest discomfort.** You can experience sharp pressure, burning, or dull pains in your chest that most often occur at night. Some people also experience fluttering in their chest.
- **Body aches.** Aches can occur anywhere in the body but are most often seen around the neck, shoulders, back, and hips.
- **Stomach issues.** Think about the Pepto-Bismol commercial—*"Nausea, heartburn, indigestion, upset stomach, diarrhea."* Plus, constipation is also quite common.

WHAT YOU CAN DO

If you are experiencing physical symptoms like those above, you should first check in with your doctor. Your body may be trying to tell you that something dangerous is happening inside your body.

After that, I recommend a few things you can do to decrease your political stress. The key is to focus on things where you have control. Anxiety flourishes in areas of our lives where we have little to no control.

Just like vowels are essential for language, the following tips are essential to improve your physical and emotional health:

- **Avoid contention.** While we will have conflict at times, we do have the power to avoid contention (heated disagreements). This may be a season where you limit contentious conversations and entertainment (including news). Read relaxing books. Watch fun movies. Invest in encouraging friendships that help you to think more broadly about topics.
- **Eat healthy.** Make sure to eat three well-rounded meals each day. Focus on fresh fruit and vegetables. Limit junk food and sugary drinks. Maybe take a cooking class to learn how to make healthy food that tastes good.
- **In bed by ten.** Sleep is foundational to our health yet is often overlooked. Set a clear bedtime so you can get eight hours of sleep. Keep electronics (TV, phones, tablets) completely out of the room to get the best sleep.
- **Outdoors.** Get outside. Exercise and fresh air are pivotal in reducing stress. While indoor exercise is also good, there's something organic about being in nature that melts stress away.
- **Unplug.** Prayer and meditation can put you into a relaxed state. Try putting your phone away for set periods of time to focus on the present. Be mindful of your sensations and dwell on things that make you grateful.

FINAL THOUGHTS

"For I know the plans I have for you," declares the
LORD, "plans to prosper you and not to harm you,
plans to give you hope and a future." (Jeremiah 29:11)

In the above verse, God is speaking through Jeremiah to give this promise to Israel. It sounds awesome, but the tough part is that he is not promising easy times just around the next corner. This is written to an exiled group that has no political power and no hope of things turning around for decades. He calls his people to thrive despite their circumstances.

God is in control. His promises do not rely on the results of any election (even if this is the most important election ever . . . at least until the next one).

Peace I leave with you; my peace I give you. I do not
give to you as the world gives. Do not let your hearts
be troubled and do not be afraid. (John 14:27)

DISCUSSION & REFLECTION

1. Consider the above list of symptoms commonly associated with anxiety. Which of these do you notice most prominently when you are under a lot of stress?

2. Think about how some sources of stress are avoidable where others are unavoidable. What are times when it's necessary to experience high levels of stress?

3. What things are helpful for you in reducing your stress levels?

4. In the past, how has stress affected your relationship with Jesus?

5. Where is God calling you to make changes in how you consume media to reduce contention and stress in your life?

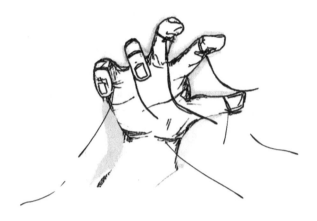

IDENTITY IN CHRIST

DAISY COCAR

Program Director of Joann's Cottage, and serves at Christ Fellowship Church & Footprint Church

I AM THE DAUGHTER OF IMMIGRANTS. In 1980 my parents escaped a civil war in their native country, finding refuge in the United States. Their story mirrors that of countless others. Immigrants and their US-born children constitute a significant portion of our population, including some 90.8 million people (about 27 percent of the US population), according to the Migration Policy Institute (2023).

Today's American culture is marked by division and partisanship. As a Christian, I have witnessed firsthand how these divisions can seep even into faith communities, distracting us from our core mission. While election outcomes are important, they are not the ultimate measure of our faith. Our true mission lies in our capacity to love. We are a people guided by the greatest commandment—to love God with all our heart, soul, and mind, and to love our neighbor as ourselves.

This love for one another proclaims to the world that we are followers of Jesus. In an era where political discourse often dominates culture, it is easy to tie our identity to a political party or a particular issue. However, as believers in Christ, at the heart of our identity lies a calling that far outweighs politics. In this divisive election season, the church can shine by demonstrating the love of Jesus. This is a love that is not contingent on personal preferences, nationality, race, or politics, but is instead grounded in the love of God.

The world is constantly trying to label us and categorize us. This makes sense, because God instilled in each of us a desire to be known, understood, and loved. Labels can foster a sense of belonging, connectedness, and purpose. This is why we often embrace them with pride. Whether as Philly fans, Americans, Latinos, feminists, pro-life advocates, or others, labels can be an important aspect of our lives. While it's acceptable to take pride in these labels, we must be vigilant not to let them overshadow our fundamental identity as followers of Jesus. Holding any identity more closely than our identity in Christ prevents us from experiencing the fullness of unity with God and his church. Therefore, we must be prepared to relinquish any identity that conflicts with our true identity in Christ.

As one of the few Latinas in my graduating high school class, I often felt different and misunderstood. Despite being US-born and fluent in English, I was identified as an ESL (English as a Second Language) student, separating me from my peers. Experiences like this bred insecurities about whether I truly belonged or could take part and excel in the same spaces as my peers. This intensified my pride as a Latina, but also fueled an internal fear that "they" were the "real Americans" who would never fully accept or value me. However, as my faith and understanding have matured, I have realized how fear and pride in an identity has sometimes obstructed my own ability to unite with those who are not like me. Although I am still a proud Latina, I now understand that without intentionally surrendering my insecurities to the Lord, I risk impeding the work he is doing in me.

Being a daughter of immigrants plays a huge part in who I am today, but it does not define who I am in the deepest sense. The example set forth by my parents was one marked by resiliency, hard work, commitment to service, and the building of God's kingdom. They arrived in this country without speaking English, with little more than a backpack, and burdened with the trauma of war. But they also had the type of faith that moves mountains. Throughout their years in ministry, I have observed my parents' relentless efforts to help other immigrants assimilate into American culture and systems. They have helped families enroll their children in school. They have provided access to English and entrepreneurship classes. They have also helped secure housing, and have facilitated access to legal resources, and other crucial services for immigrants. Their work has demonstrated to me that love is not just a feeling but an active service to God and others.

The United States has provided a pathway for my family, instilling in me a deep love for this nation. Although I am a proud American, a New Yorker, a daughter of immigrants, and a social worker, I am learning that my foremost identity is as a daughter of God on mission with him. This belief in God's overarching command to love, show hospitality, and care for others transcends our cultural identities.

In the years Jesus walked this earth, he was not concerned with earthly political power. He was mission-focused, fully aware of his identity and purpose. He came to this world to bridge the gap, sacrificing himself in love for all of humanity. As followers of Christ our primary identity is rooted in Jesus. Any identity other than our faith in Christ should be secondary and held tentatively. Jesus teaches in John chapter 17 that we are not of this world and that our ultimate allegiance is to him. He has appointed us as his ambassadors, tasked to lead lives that reflect his character. He longs for our actions and words to testify to his presence in us. We should resist the seeds of division sown by party lines and political ideologies. Differences are inevitable, but division is a choice. Professing love for Jesus while harboring hatred toward our brothers and sisters contradicts the essence of the Great Commission and the love we are mandated to spread. Current issues must not obstruct our mission to share the love of Jesus.

We are called to fulfill the commandment to love as Jesus has loved us. Christ's love is a force powerful enough to break down human barriers and transform paradigms. As the light and salt of the earth we should actively engage in his mission, emulating Jesus' actions of healing the sick, raising the dead, feeding the hungry, caring for the marginalized, and forgiving sinners. It's crucial to relinquish any part of our identity that obstructs the light of Jesus within us from reaching others. Proverbs 31:8–9 teaches us the importance of living as a people who shine the light of God. The Scripture says, "Open your mouth for the mute, for the rights of all who are destitute. Open your mouth, judge righteously, defend the rights of the poor and needy."

In today's materialistic and power-hungry culture, Christianity stands as a countercultural force, advocating for the needs of others over selfish desires. Philippians 2:2–4 ESV says,

> Complete my joy by being of the same mind, having the same love, being in full accord and of one mind. Do nothing from selfish ambition or conceit, but in humility count others more significant than yourselves. Let each of you look not only to his own interests, but also to the interests of others.

The problems we see in today's culture are nothing new; we are dealing with the same evil that has always existed. Sin is at the root of all forms of oppression, injustice, and brokenness. Sin is our enemy, not people who disagree with us. Our battle is spiritual, against dark forces, not against individuals or communities. Viewing others through a lens of compassion and recognizing them as God's image-bearers empowers us to be his ambassadors. In this role, we convey the truth of Jesus' sacrifice and his mission to reconcile people with God.

The words of Micah 6:8 hold profound significance for us today. Micah, a prophet chosen by God, confronted the moral and spiritual decline of Israel. He was deeply troubled by the societal decay and the suffering caused by corrupt leaders, who enriched themselves at the expense of the poor. Micah's message, which rebuked Israel and Judah for sins like oppression, corruption, exploitation, greed, and pride, echoes many of the same issues we face today. Sin was pervasive, and religious practices had become more about ritual than heartfelt worship. Micah posed a poignant question, "What does the LORD require of you?" And the response was clear: "To act justly and to love mercy and to walk humbly with your God."

As we navigate the often-turbulent waters of an election season, my faith compels me to view politics not as a battlefield of division, but as a field ripe for sowing seeds of love and unity. This is an opportunity for us to extend grace, to do what is right, to judge fairly, show mercy, practice humility, and to approach others with curiosity and empathy. Rather than viewing others through labels, let's hold firmly to our core identity and focus on Christ and his kingdom. Let us be firm in our faith, knowing that Christ is King, regardless of the political outcome.

In this spirit, I urge each of us to take the following steps toward fostering unity:

1. **Engage in respectful dialogue.** Make a conscious effort to listen and engage with those who have different political views. Strive to understand their perspectives without judgment and share your own views with kindness and respect.

2. **Serve together.** Actively look for opportunities to serve in your community alongside people of different backgrounds and beliefs. Working together toward a common goal can build bridges and break down barriers of division.

3. **Pray for unity.** Regularly pray for unity within the church and among believers. Ask God to heal divisions and to guide us in living out his love and grace in every interaction.

4. **Educate yourself and others.** Seek to understand the issues that divide us and educate others on the importance of unity in Christ. Use your platform, no matter how big or small, to advocate for love and understanding.

5. **Model Christ's love.** In all things, let your words and actions reflect the love of Christ. Be a living example of his unconditional love and forgiveness, showing others that our identity in him transcends all earthly divisions.

By embracing these steps, we can contribute to a culture of unity and love, reflecting the heart of the gospel in our communities and beyond. Let us move forward with a commitment to be peacemakers, remembering that our ultimate allegiance is to Christ, who calls us to unity in his name.

DISCUSSION & REFLECTION

1. The essay emphasizes the centrality of love in the Christian faith. How does Jesus exemplify this love through his teachings and actions, and what can we learn from his example?

2. What are some examples of societal pressures or influences that may lead individuals to prioritize certain identities over their identity in Christ?

3. How can individuals ensure that their primary allegiance remains to Christ amid the challenges posed by political polarization and societal pressures?

4. The essay touches on the idea of viewing others through a lens of compassion and recognizing them as God's image-bearers. How can this perspective influence our interactions with those who are different or hold differing opinions or lifestyles?

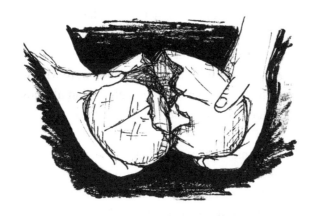

IN REMEMBRANCE OF ME

NOEL GENIZA

Founding Pastor of International Christian Fellowship

I WAS BORN IN THE PREDOMINANTLY Catholic nation of the Philippines. In third grade I was invited to celebrate my first Holy Communion. My religion teacher gathered our class and took us to the church near our school. At that time, I didn't understand the meaning or purpose of Communion. When we arrived, I was told that the priest would place the wafer in my mouth, and that I should let it dissolve on my tongue. I was also instructed that I *must not* chew it because it was the actual body of Christ. Another person said, "If the wafer sticks to the palate of your mouth it means you have many sins!" What do you think happened? *Of course,* the wafer stuck like glue to the top of my mouth!

Although the wafer tasted strange, what really concerned me was the number of sins I must have—the stickiness of the wafer indicated that there were quite a few. After that, I avoided taking Communion whenever I attended Mass. But there were times I couldn't evade it because my friends were with me, and I didn't want to be left alone feeling guilty about all those sins. Every time I took Communion the wafer continued to stick to my mouth.

When I became a born-again believer and follower of Jesus Christ in 1982, I was introduced to a different way of partaking Communion. My new church served real bread from a loaf that was cut into little square pieces. They also passed out cups of grape juice. This was different for me, because in my Catholic church we were not given the juice. I have to say, one thing I liked about this was that I could finally chew the bread!

The pastor explained to me that the bread symbolizes the body of Christ broken on our behalf and the juice symbolizes the blood of Jesus Christ poured out as a sin offering. Everything began to make sense to me in new ways as I continued to study the Scriptures.

Since then, I have learned to freely take Communion without worrying about how many sins I have committed. I now understand that Jesus paid for all my sins through his death and resurrection. His body was punished and bruised, and his blood was poured out at the cross as the atoning sacrifice for my sins. Because of this understanding, the Lord's Supper has become increasingly meaningful to me. And now as a pastor I have the privilege of leading our congregation in our monthly remembrance of the Lord's Supper.

Just like my first pastors taught me, I always quote 1 Corinthians 11:23–29:

> For I received from the Lord what I also passed on to you: The Lord Jesus, on the night he was betrayed, took bread, and when he had given thanks, he broke it and said, "This is my body, which is for you; do this in remembrance of me." In the same way, after supper he took the cup, saying, "This cup is the new covenant in my blood; do this, whenever you drink it, in remembrance of me." For whenever you eat this bread and drink this cup, you proclaim the Lord's death until he comes. So then, whoever eats the bread or drinks the cup of the Lord in an unworthy manner will be guilty of sinning against the body and blood of the Lord. Everyone ought to examine themselves before they eat of the bread and drink from the cup. For those who eat and drink without discerning the body of Christ eat and drink judgment on themselves.

Over the years, as I have read this passage, I have been left with a question. What does it mean to partake in an *unworthy* manner? When I first became a Christian, my pastors taught that verse 27 specifically discourages unbelievers from participating in Communion. The verse talks about eating the bread and drinking the wine in an "unworthy manner." I was taught that anyone who has not yet received Jesus in their lives but who partakes in Communion is taking into themselves the curse of God.

When I became a pastor, I began to wonder if that is what Paul really had in mind. I looked at the text again and asked, Was Paul really talking primarily about unbelievers? Didn't Paul write 1 Corinthians to *believers* in Corinth? If this is the case, then the primary warning can't be about unbelievers. So, what exactly was Paul thinking about when he warned the early church not to eat in an "unworthy manner"?

The larger context, found in verses 17–22, sheds light on what Paul probably meant. He was addressing the abuse of the Lord's Supper that was taking place in the church of Corinth. There were divisions among them, specifically between the rich and the poor. Evidently, there was a rift between those who had much and those who had little. Their meals were meant to be times of unity and hospitality, instead they were becoming divisive.

The Corinthian Christians probably held a full weekly meal together. Part of the meal would have been specifically remembering Jesus' atoning sacrifice. One of the problems seems to have been that those who brought more food feasted compared to those who were only able to bring a little to share. Additionally, poorer individuals usually work longer hours or undesirable shifts. Apparently the more affluent members of the church did not think it was worth waiting for everyone to arrive before they took the best portions for themselves. As a result, some of the Corinthian believers were hungry while some overate and even got drunk. This is the "unworthy manner" that Paul rebuked in verse 27.

When Jesus instituted the Last Supper in the gospel of Luke, he particularly emphasized one thing—that the disciples do it in *remembrance* of him. The disciples had no idea what was going to happen that night. For them, it was another yearly Passover meal. They were commemorating the event in Israel's history when the angel of death passed over any Israelite house with the blood of the lamb on their doors. They were remembering that night when God delivered them from slavery out of Egypt. And now Jesus was telling them to take and eat the bread, which was his body, in remembrance of him—to remember him as the new Passover Lamb who takes away the sins of the world.

The twelve disciples had their own share of acting in an "unworthy manner." Do you remember when they fought among themselves about who would be the greatest in Jesus' kingdom? They were far from perfect. They even abandoned Jesus that very night! And yet, Jesus accepted them and shared that supper with them. And Jesus taught them, "Do this in remembrance of me."

Around the table that evening sat a group of people who, apart from Jesus, would not have been friends. At the table sat Matthew the tax collector and Simon the Zealot. In the flesh, these men were rivals, even enemies. But their relationship with Jesus drew them together. The sacrifice of Christ transformed these two enemies into brothers. The sacrifice of Jesus continues to do the same miraculous work today. Notice how the word *union* sits at the core of Comm*union*. Communion brings together the rich and the poor, tax collectors and zealots, males and females, Jews and Gentiles, and even political rivals—all at the feet of Jesus.

This precious sacrament is all about Jesus. It's not about who we are by earthly measures or what socio-economic status we came from. Nor is the Lord's Supper about our differences in culture, or the color of our skin, or our political inclinations. We eat and drink *in remembrance of Jesus*. He alone is Lord.

During this divisive political season, each time we take Communion, we are invited to remember that we worship the one true King. His kingdom is not contained by any earthly political party, and he makes spiritual siblings and ministry partners out of rivals.

I am learning more and more to treat the Lord's Supper as an invitation from Jesus to have supper with him. When Jesus had meals with sinners, the religious people didn't always like it. But Jesus says in Revelation 3:20, "Here I am! I stand at the door and knock. If anyone hears my voice and opens the door, I will come in and eat with that person, and they with me." The Lord's Supper is an invitation for all to come to sit and eat with him. After all, he is the true Passover Lamb who takes away the sins of the world.

DISCUSSION & REFLECTION

1. How does the practice of Communion remind us to love our brothers and sisters?

2. How does the cross inform the way we forgive and extend grace to others?

3. How did Jesus use the imagery of his broken body and shed blood to break down human walls of division?

4. Is there a broken or strained relationship in your life that you can pray for healing and reconciliation today?

WHAT'S LOVE GOT TO DO WITH IT?

DARRELL C. BROWN JR.
Senior Pastor of Rhema Ministries International

WHAT'S LOVE GOT TO DO With It? is a 1993 biopic made about the life of the legendary singer Tina Turner. I like this question. "What's love got to do with it?" As a local church pastor and community leader, I believe this question is exactly what Christians should be asking as we head into another bitter and divisive election cycle.

Yes, there are significant and real differences of opinions and ideologies that people feel and hold strongly. But throughout this political season Christians have a unique opportunity to embody love, and even embrace with friendship and compassion those who vote differently. As believers in the Lord Jesus

Christ, we are called to love all people regardless of their political affiliation.

The foundation of Christian love lies in the teaching of Jesus Christ. The night before his crucifixion Jesus said to his disciples, "A new command I give you: Love one another. As I have loved you, so you must love one another. By this everyone will know that you are my disciples, if you love one another" (John 13:34–35).

This love extends beyond personal preferences, opinions, and political beliefs. The Bible teaches us that God created all people, and every individual is made in his image (Genesis 1:27). This is why Christians believe so strongly in love of neighbor. We are called to embody the selfless love demonstrated by Christ himself. That includes loving people who hold different political convictions than our own.

The love of Christ compels us to love others beyond the limitations of our own biases and prejudices. Granted, this can be difficult because we live in such a broken world. And people can be very rude and mean sometimes! What does true, Jesus-shaped love look like when living in our earthly, fallen society?

For example, what if we were to glimpse two Christians in the deep American South during the 1960s and see these two believers waiting for the same bus, heading in the same direction? Both Christians may have had the same foundational belief that Jesus Christ is Lord, but one was forced to sit in the back of the bus while the other had the option of sitting wherever they liked. The one would feel belittled. The other may have felt exalted, giving that individual the experience of an elite status over their Christian brother.

So, you can understand why they would vote differently. Similar situations have so often resulted in tension and anger.

Understandably, it seems that strongly held political persuasions are often birthed out of our own personal experiences and contexts. However, in Christ, there is a bridge of love that can connect us regardless of our personal experiences, cultural differences, race, gender, and ethnicity. As fellow believers of Jesus, it is crucial for us to develop the skill set of agreeing to disagree on secondary or tertiary issues. We do not have to be divided on every single issue we disagree about. Those who know the love of Jesus are tasked to teach this current and future generation the true meaning of the love of God and how it brings about the ministry of reconciliation (2 Corinthians 5:18–19).

Is the love of Jesus the key to this ministry of reconciliation? *What's love got to do with it?* How can the love of God help us bridge the gaps that so often divide us?

John 3:16 says, "For God so loved the world that he gave his one and only Son, that whoever believes in him shall not perish but have eternal life."

I believe there is no greater Scripture in all the Bible than John 3:16. This beautiful passage summarizes God's remarkable love for humanity, and it reveals the way God brings about salvation. This Scripture gives us the great promise of God's saving work. This is the greatest gift ever given to mankind.

Unfortunately, in today's culture, the word *love* is used so commonly and carelessly that it seems to have lost some of its value and its true, sacrificial meaning. In English we use the same word to describe our relationship with pizza as we do with our own child. *"I love pizza." "I love my child."* Do you see the problem? These are not the same things, and I don't feel the same way about pizza that I do about my child!

God's love is different than how we feel about last night's dinner. John 3:16 doesn't mean that God loves the world like I love pizza. The Greeks had several words they used to convey different types of love. The word translated as "loved" in John 3:16 is the Greek word *agape. Agape* is the unmerited, gracious, lavish, unconditional love of God. This is the kind of love Christians are supposed to emulate. First, we receive this love from God through Jesus, then we share that same love with others.

Love is who God is. As Christians, you and I have already received his love, and are learning to receive it more each day. With the Lord's help, we can love others more tomorrow than we do today. While human love often fluctuates based on our mood, behavior, or lack of obedience to Jesus, that is not the case with the love of God. His love never changes or wavers. In Christ, we are perfectly and fully loved.

The *agape* love of God is unconditional. He loves all people. Jesus says in John 3:16, "For God so loved the world that he gave his one and only Son, that whoever believes in him shall not perish but have eternal life."

In this statement the word translated into English as the word "world" is the Greek word *cosmos. Cosmos* includes the entirety and totality of humanity. This leaves no one outside the love of God. God loves Democrats and Republicans. He loves conservatives and liberals. God loves Baptists and Methodists. He loves White and Black, males and females. God loves the whole world.

John 3:16 also teaches us that God loves the world so much that "he gave his one and only Son." This truth lets us know that this *agape* love is a self-sacrificial love for the benefit of others. Jesus, the perfect Lamb of God, who takes away the sins of the world, willingly laid down his own life as a sin offering to redeem all those who come to faith in him.

Just from John 3:16 we can see that God perfectly loves the whole world, and desires to rescue everyone through the saving work of his beloved Son Jesus Christ. If we have received Jesus Christ as Lord and Savior, we are called to love others in the same way.

So, *what's love got to do with it?* Everything! I believe the love of Jesus has *everything* to do with and to speak to this moment in our culture. We are Christians living through another politically divisive season. The love of Jesus motivates us to act without prejudice or discrimination, for God's love is a love without the limits of man.

In this political season we must look to the example our heavenly Father has set for us. God has given us the perfect example to follow by demonstrating his own perfect love for us through sending his only Son to reconcile us to himself. Despite all our unique differences and all our brokenness and sin, Jesus still loved us with a perfect, *agape* love. "While we were still sinners, Christ died for us" (Romans 5:8).

In Jesus, God has given us the perfect example to follow. If he can bridge the gap between himself and us, then his perfect love can teach us to build bridges between those we might politically disagree with.

What's love to got to do with it? If we are honest and humble enough to look to the example of our King Jesus, love has *everything* to do with it.

DISCUSSION & REFLECTION

1. Reflecting on the examples given in the article, how can personal experiences shape political beliefs and voting choices? How can Christians find common ground and bridge the gap of love despite our political differences?

2. In exploring the distinction between worldly love and God's love (*agape* love) mentioned in the article, how can Christians prioritize and emulate God's love in their political engagement and discussions?

3. When you reflect on the statement *What's love got to do with it?* in the context of politics and the Christian faith, how can love play a transformative role in addressing political division and promoting unity?

BEST PRACTICES FOR SOCIAL MEDIA USAGE DURING THE ELECTION CYCLE

JESSE HOFFMAN

Associate Pastor at Coventry Church

I T DOESN'T TAKE ME LONG to think of a time where trouble began in the comment sections online. In these memories, sometimes I was the one involved in the squabble; sometimes I was snacking on my imaginary popcorn while reading a verbal brawl between impassioned keyboard warriors. Name calling, logical fallacies, and immoral arguments often occur in said online debates, but that doesn't stop many of us from diving headfirst into the flames of the comment sections, thinking we can singlehandedly vanquish our "opponents'" arguments. Ironically, in the process of engaging with these "internet villains" we can become villains ourselves by forsaking the principles of the faith we claim to hold. This is just one of the examples of why we need to consider our social media usage so carefully.

Social media is a tool many of us use frequently, ranging from a couple of times a week to multiple times a day. Social media can be helpful or harmful. It allows us easy access to the digital world but challenges us to use self-control in a way previous generations never had to. The purpose of this article is to help Christians learn about social media and how to handle it during the election cycle. To do this we need to first understand the social media business; second, see the ways social media can be unhealthy; and third, recognize how we as Christians can use social media in a healthy, life-giving manner. These principles will equip us to thrive as believers and represent Christ both online and off.

UNDERSTANDING THE BUSINESS

To understand why social media is so divisive, and often destructive, we need to first understand the platforms' basic business tactic, which is getting you to click stuff.[1] We may naively think the tech companies running our social media platforms are benevolently gifting us with a free outlet to see fun cat videos, share pictures of the family, and get news updates, but that is often the farthest thing from the truth!

A major issue we face when using social media is that divisive content sells better and gets more clicks than the cute family photo you shared over the holidays. CSIS Journalism Bootcamp, an initiative connecting journalists, policy experts, and multimedia producers, writes, "Companies face a difficult business incentive: content that shows more extreme sources tends to get more engagement."[2] Unfortunately, this encourages the sharing of extreme and/or misleading news. As Christians, we should know that Satan is seeking to bring division, fear, and anger to God's world and the church. The Word of God says in Romans 12:18 ESV, "If possible, so far as it depends on you, live peaceably with all." How can we live peaceably with others when we are exposed to things that constantly provoke us to anger or are untrue?

Tragically, because of the division sown by extreme voices on social media, people often struggle to see the "other" as a fellow human made in God's image. As followers of Jesus, we don't believe that all beliefs are right or equal. However, the people holding different beliefs are no less made in God's image and deserving of the treatment Jesus would offer them. Even to those living in blatant sin, Jesus lovingly showed the truth while never forcing them to adopt it.

UNHEALTHY SOCIAL MEDIA

As we seek to represent Jesus Christ with integrity, we need to avoid unhealthy ways of using social media. One of the reasons I wrote this article is because I have learned from my past experiences what unhealthy social media usage looks like and how it affects people, including myself. I would say that irresponsible social media usage almost always includes elements of the following points.

1. **We allow our focus to drift from God and onto things of the world.** Often this is a gradual process formed by a habit of getting on our phones or computers too frequently. In my own experience, being on a screen too much makes it harder to think of spiritual realities since I'm overly focused on either work or leisure.

Have you seen what's happening in the world right now? Watching the news 24/7 and I have no idea how God is okay with this . . . —@NewsheadNed

91

2. **We behave differently online because we think we are unaccountable for what we say.** Screens cause us to disassociate ourselves from the real-world consequences of what we say, but that is impossible. We should be even more careful online because anything we type has the potential to be made available to the entire world. Next time you're thinking about responding to someone online, think about saying it out loud in front of Jesus.

> *Dante, you're a lying sack of crap because you know I never said that, but you idiotically spread the darn lie anyways. Go burn.—@AngryAmy*

3. **We fall into the trap of "confirmation bias" and believe anything that aligns with what we want to hear.** There are many people out there with an agenda and will intentionally manipulate the way they present facts. It is irresponsible to believe (or disbelieve) something without giving it some investigation. As Christians, we want to be acutely aware of what we spread to avoid disseminating or believing lies.

> *I found proof the government is hiding the secret bunker of alien technologies that were used to build the pyramids! Read here!—@ConspiracyCory*

There have been times I fell into every one of those past points. I understand the desire to reply or comment on someone's post in a way you would never engage with them in person. I have felt the temptation to worry about political situations more than I trust Jesus. I have believed headlines that ended up being mere controversial opinions. Through all this, I have learned what the Bible has to say about interacting with others. Proverbs 10:19 ESV says, "When words are many, transgression is not lacking, but whoever restrains his lips is prudent."

Prudence means *"showing care and thought for the future,"* so, by being careful with what we say online instead of saying the first thing that comes to mind, we show care for the future. We build a social currency by treating others with respect, which will make our job as representatives of God's kingdom easier (2 Corinthians 5:19).

HEALTHY SOCIAL MEDIA

As we seek to represent Christ well, pointing to him both online and offline, it is important to consider how to use social media in a healthy manner. Some people decide to completely rid themselves of all social media presence because of its unhealthy characteristics. However, this isn't the call on every Christian's life. Those who engage others online can learn how to use social media in a Christ-honoring manner.

1. **When needed, take a break.** The Bible says in James 1:19 ESV, "Know this, my beloved brothers: let every person be quick to hear, slow to speak, slow to anger." If you sense frustration building from what you see or read online, take a break. Put down the phone or turn off the computer for a while. When I am getting upset about injustices from around the world or from others' comments, I turn off the phone and retreat for a while. Refraining from social media for a set time to reorient your focus on God is also recommended if you sense too much negativity when you use social media.

2. **Keep Jesus first.** Remember the call for believers to "seek first the kingdom of God (Matthew 6:33 ESV). The internet gives us great opportunities to grow our understanding of God through interacting with other Christians; it's not all doom and gloom! God's kingdom is on the move, and we can use social media to help spread his message.

93

3. **Do not be afraid.** This is one of the most repeated commands in the Bible. God knows what is going on in the world and is always at work. Jesus, living under the reign of the Roman Empire, did not worry about what was to come. Christians must seek ways to be Christ-like examples to the world, sometimes through the political system, but never at the expense of our identity as ambassadors of the kingdom of God.

4. **Remember the "why."** Knowing the purpose of why we use social media is also helpful in using it properly. Are we on it just for entertainment, for news, for friends, or something else? Particularly now, with elections on the horizon, we need to know why we're online. So, why are you using social media? Is it to waste time, entertain yourself, or numb your pain, or can social media be a way for you to share the love of Jesus with others?

Let us use this opportunity of connecting with the world to better represent Jesus to an even broader audience!

DISCUSSION & REFLECTION

1. What is your purpose in using social media?

2. In what ways has your social media usage reflected your personal convictions and worldview?

3. Are there specific social media platforms or situations online that make healthy usage harder?

4. How can you use social media in a God-honoring way?

ORIENTING TO JESUS
IN THE TENSION

CORY ERMOLD

Pastor of Worship & Creative Arts at Mstar Church

ES MISÉRABLES BY VICTOR HUGO has captivated the hearts of its audience for decades. The incredible retelling of France's history as depicted through the story's various characters creates a profoundly human and relatable story. This is evidenced in its multi-generational popularity, making it one of the most beloved books and musicals in the world.

The story opens in the year 1815 with Jean Valjean, an incarcerated French peasant, being released after spending nineteen years in prison. His crime was stealing a loaf of bread to save his sister's starving child. Valjean's story unfolds against a backdrop of societal unrest, echoing the deep-seated conflicts between the French government and the commoners. The tale highlights the moral and ethical dilemmas created in a turbulent world. We are drawn into Jean Valjean's journey as he wrestles with the myriad tensions he feels both inwardly and outwardly. Though the story never wraps these tensions up in a neat bow, Valjean's faith allows him to come to a place of rest and contentment, even amid all these difficulties.

Jean Valjean's journey is a remarkably human and relatable story. It's a journey of pain and love, one that we all must travel. Jesus walked this same journey when he took on flesh and became man. He stepped into the same kinds of trials and struggles that we face, demonstrating perfectly how to lean into the tension that life inevitably provides.

Life often presents struggles that tug at the very essence of who we are. They generate tensions that can lead to pain, chaos, and turmoil in our mental, emotional, spiritual, and physical health. This same tension can propel us forward into a greater understanding of ourselves and the world around us. Whenever we encounter these moments of tension in our lives, we stand at a crossroads, faced with a decision. Do we retreat from the tension, opt for evasion, and sidestep the pain? Or do we lean into the tension and discover the grace waiting within? Tension allows for us to orient ourselves toward a Father who patiently waits to guide us through those moments. This is the very work that God wants to do in our lives. Jesus, working in and through the tensions we face in a broken world, desires to orient our hearts, souls, and minds to his kingdom.

INWARD ORIENTATION TOWARD GOD IS THE FOUNDATION OF SPIRITUAL ALIGNMENT

The portrayal of Jesus' life in the Gospels consistently reveals tension. He exemplified how we are to live in and through tension, abiding with the Father through it all. In Matthew 26:39

we find Jesus in the garden of Gethsemane speaking to his Father, and crying out, "My Father, if it is possible, may this cup be taken from me. Yet not as I will, but as you will." Jesus wrestled. And he teaches us how to wrestle with God through the tensions of our own lives. At times, Jesus was frustrated, misunderstood, accused, and even betrayed. Yet in his question to God, Jesus shows how alignment through submission tips the scale from reality to the fulfilled outcome.

Moreover, as Jesus is crucified in Matthew 27:46, his cry, "My God, my God, why have you forsaken me?" reverberates with the anguish of abandonment and internal strife. This moment highlights the stark tension between Christ's embodied vulnerability and the divine authority he still fully holds. It illustrates a transition from the depths of utter desolation to asserting his ultimate dominion, even as he approaches his last breath, signifying the defeat of the world's curse. On the cross, an internal and external tension that gives way to the kingdom of God is being birthed. When we learn to follow Jesus' example of finding internal orientation in the will of the Father, we also experience alignment with the heart of God.

OUTWARD ORIENTATION TOWARD JESUS' KINGDOM MANIFESTS HIS DIVINE PRINCIPLES IN THE WORLD

"Seek first his kingdom and his righteousness, and all these things will be given to you as well" (Matthew 6:33). This Scripture is surrounded by text that can be summarized by this statement: Do not worry (Matthew 6:25–34). Life's external pressures, ranging from family dynamics and financial worries to divisive political seasons, to packed schedules and career demands, are ever-present challenges. This raises the question: What does it truly mean to "seek the kingdom" while navigating daily life without worry? Is it possible to actively pursue God's kingdom amid our bustling routines? Internal conflicts are one aspect, but when combined with the external stresses surrounding us, they can lead us into a state of distraction.

Only by orienting ourselves toward God can we bear fruit amid all this external turmoil. C.S. Lewis once remarked in a sermon that the pursuit of knowledge, or any goal, often occurs under less-than-ideal circumstances. He noted, "If we let ourselves, we shall always be waiting for some distraction or other to end before we can really get down to our work. The only people who achieve much are those who want knowledge so badly that they seek it while the conditions are still unfavourable. Favourable conditions never come."[1] Lewis acknowledges that there are times when external pressures are overwhelming, requiring almost superhuman strength to overcome. These moments occur in both times of peace and conflict, urging us to do the best we can under the circumstances. When we seek first the kingdom of God, even (or especially) when the external pressures of the world are pressing down on us, we can, like Jesus, manifest the principles of God to the world.

RELATIONAL ALIGNMENT IS THE FRUIT OF ORIENTATION TOWARD GOD AND HIS KINGDOM

Throughout the internal and external challenges faced by Jesus, a recurring theme emerges—*maintaining alignment with God.* Our alignment with God directly influences our capacity to endure tension peacefully. There is a deep connection between the state of one's heart and their ability to navigate tension in a Christ-like manner. Love serves as the core driving force fueling both Jesus' ministry and the broader narrative of the Scriptures. John emphasizes this in 1 John 4:7, stating, "Dear friends, let us love one another, for love comes from God. Everyone who loves has been born of God and knows God," further highlighting a few verses later that God *is* love. Perhaps love is the most important fruit of orienting ourselves to God and to his kingdom around us.

In his final moments in the musical version of *Les Misérables*, Jean Valjean's dying thoughts are sung, "to love another person is to see the face of God."[2] This realization not only marks the pinnacle of Valjean's spiritual journey but also underscores the transformative power of love and the divine potential of aligning our inner convictions with our outward actions. Valjean's life, marred by hardship and injustice, initially steered him toward bitterness and hatred. However, his journey led him to an inward orientation toward a higher moral compass, and his outward actions reflecting this change. "Do you hear the people sing, singing the song of angry men"[3] still has a melody that is alive in today's society. Let's learn how to sing, along with Valjean, "to love another person is to see the face of God."

It is these very tensions which allow the opportunities for us to orient ourselves toward a Father who patiently waits to guide us through a fractious world. In Christ, our internal and external tensions give way to the kingdom of God being birthed.

DISCUSSION & REFLECTION

1. Reflecting on Jesus' moments of internal and external tension, how can you apply his example of alignment with God's will to your own moments of struggle or decision-making?

2. Considering the concept of "seeking the kingdom" amid daily stresses, what practical steps can you take to prioritize God's kingdom in your busy life?

3. In your relationships, how can adopting a stance of love and forgiveness, as emphasized by Jesus and Paul, help navigate conflicts and foster deeper connections?

4. How has your understanding of God's love and kingdom influenced your approach to life's tensions, and what changes might you make to reflect this more fully in your actions and attitudes?

DEAR GEN Z, BOOMERS, & EVERYONE IN-BETWEEN

REGAN SIGOURNEY

Ministry Leadership at Chesmont Young Adults,
Parker Ford Church, & a Special Education teacher.

DID YOU KNOW THAT ALEXANDER Hamilton was just twenty years old when he was promoted to Lieutenant Colonel during the Revolutionary War? Or that Mozart was twelve when he composed his first opera? Amelia Earhart was only twenty-five when she set the altitude record in her Kinner Airster biplane! Did you know that Alexander the Great was eighteen years old when he began his conquest of the ancient world?

Each of these historic figures achieved some of their most influential accomplishments in their teenage or young adult years. And they all share something else. Hamilton led under the guidance of George Washington, Mozart created alongside his father, Earhart was trained by her mentor, Neta Snook, and Alexander the Great spent his early teenage years in the company of Aristotle. Each had intergenerational relationships that contributed to their formative years in a way that led to some of their most significant historical accomplishments.

In 2022, Encore.org published the results of a study completed with NORC at the University of Chicago in an article called "Cogeneration."[1] The study surveyed Gen Z, Millennials, Gen X, and Boomers about their desire to bridge generational gaps and solve societal problems together. Results of the study found that 96.4 percent of people agreed that working across generations can help America better solve its problems. And 93.7 percent agreed that working across generations can reduce divisions in our society. This study showed that people across generations truly desired to work together for the betterment of society.

America is inching closer to another election. Any push for multigenerational unity will likely be thrown out the window during the next political election cycle. Political candidates often use their platforms to pit generations against each other. Different political parties appeal to one generation over and against others. And when the election comes to an end, in their wake, they've left an even greater generational divide.

We, as the body of Christ, can do things differently. During a time when politicians often capitalize on the conflict and differences between generations, can we, as the church, walk in multigenerational unity instead? Within the church, both older and younger people share responsibility in valuing unity across generational lines.

Each generation has strengths and weaknesses. Gen Z is ambitious, craving authenticity and justice; they're tech savvy and confident. But they're also impulsive, struggle with entitlement, and often prefer comfort over doing something hard, even when it's something good.

Older generations are incredibly hard workers; they're disciplined and loyal, and their life experience gives them invaluable wisdom and perspective. But they can also be resistant to change, focused on maintaining control, and wary of the ways society is progressing, sometimes to the point of cynicism. As we work to bridge the gap, each generation must be humbly aware of their shortcomings and hopeful about the ways we can work together.

In the spirit of fostering healthy, intergenerational communication, below is a short open letter written to both Gen Z and to older generations.

Dear Gen Z,

We are growing up in a post-Christian, tradition-skeptical, hyper-independent society that's trying its best to convince us that the older generations are all that's standing in the way of the society we deserve. This deception is so dangerous to the unity that Christ calls us to. When we think about walking in unity through this tension, we must think about how we belong to one another as the body of Christ.

One of the most detrimental lies culture feeds our generation is that the only person we can rely on is ourselves. In truth, the one person we can rely on is Jesus. He calls us to live in community and belong to one another just as he belonged to his Father. Isolating ourselves and our generation from the gifts and wisdom that abound in intergenerational community would be detrimental to the kingdom of Jesus.

When Jesus began building his community of disciples, two critical things happened. In the book of Matthew, it says, "As Jesus was walking beside the Sea of Galilee, he saw two brothers, Simon called Peter and his brother Andrew. They were casting a net into the lake, for they were fishermen. 'Come follow me,' Jesus said, 'and I will send you out to fish for people.' At once they left their nets and followed him" (Matthew 4:18–20). First, Jesus sought them out and told them to follow him. But even more relevant to Gen Z, the disciples submitted and made the choice to follow, and in following, belong. They left what was comfortable and easy and chose to step into community with Jesus. Jesus has called us to follow and belong too. Gen Z needs to fight against the "do it myself" culture and submit to the truth that there is abundance and life when we choose to belong to Jesus and his multigenerational body.

Dear Older Generations,

Culture is telling you to write Gen Z off as a lost cause. Let's talk about the gifts that this generation brings to the table. Some of Gen Z's trademark characteristics are their tenacity, drive, and passion. This younger generation is already overflowing with social media influencers, teenage entrepreneurs, young-adult activists, and community leaders. And the oldest members of Gen Z haven't even turned thirty yet!

Gen Z is hardwired for purpose, and even better, they desire to see their purpose have an impact. Political parties have recognized this quality in Gen Z and are targeting their campaigns to entice the newest group of voters. So why hasn't the church recognized this quality as something worthwhile? Or if they have recognized it, why isn't there a sense of urgency in the church to equip Gen Z in using this tenacity and passion to further the kingdom of Jesus?

Jesus didn't just call the disciples, have them follow him, and then use their submission as an opportunity to have twelve groupies—he equipped them and used them. Jesus could've *walked around teaching, healing, feeding, and performing miracles all on his own, but he didn't. It was customary during the time of Jesus for religious training to start at a young age, which means it was likely that most of Jesus' disciples were teenagers or young adults—and he still used them! Jesus often sent the disciples out in pairs, and one of the pairs that he consistently equipped was Peter, believed to be the oldest disciple, and John, believed to be the youngest. Jesus saw the necessity of multigenerational relationships. Christ's example should be the church's model for approaching Gen Z. There's an entire generation lined up and waiting for Jesus' call to "follow me." The church should be the first people going to meet them where they are and giving them purpose for the kingdom of Jesus.*

A CALL TO COMMUNITY

So, what do we do? How do we walk in multigenerational unity? Here are three simple ways that older and emerging generations can walk this out together.

1. **Ask questions.** Talk about the value of the old and the prospect of the new. Older generations are living in a world that looks almost nothing like how they've lived for much of their lives. Gen Z is still trying to figure out their role in that world. Ask each other what it feels like to be a part of a specific generation and what that means for their relationship with Jesus, the church, and other generations. Stop allowing a generational label to determine our opinions of each other before we ask any questions. Sit down across from one another, ask tough questions, and listen purposefully to the answers.

2. **Be with one other.** Jesus is our model for all relationships. We should do what he did. Jesus was intentional about how he walked in community with his disciples. He met them where they were, he ate with them, taught them, learned from

them, grieved with them, and rejoiced with them. Jesus washed the feet of his disciples and served them with humility in a way that so beautifully portrayed his love and deep sense of belonging to them. Where Jesus was, his disciples were. People of all ages need to help break down generational walls and make a determined effort to simply be with one another.

3. **Be okay with change.** Tradition should be valued and truth should be proclaimed, but a spirit of control stifles the movement of the Holy Spirit. Jesus doesn't call us to conform to culture, but he does call us to walk humbly with one another in love. When we walk in intergenerational relationships, humility and love will sometimes mean change. Humility and love often requires submission and honor. That might mean Gen Z walking in submission to the wisdom of older generations, or older generations engaging with new perspectives from Gen Z. Change, when it is covered in the love and the leading of the Holy Spirit, can be one of the greatest blessings to the kingdom of Jesus and the body of Christ.

The song "Hymn of Heaven" by Phil Wickham sings, "And on that day, we join the resurrection and stand beside the heroes of the faith. With one voice, a thousand generations, sing 'Worthy is the Lamb who was slain.'"[2] What a beautiful day that will be. Let's dive into that now. Amid divisiveness, let's stand beside one another, all generations joined together, using one voice to proclaim the glory of our King.

DISCUSSION & REFLECTION

Sit down with someone from a different generation than you, and ask them:

1. What about your generation makes you feel proudest? How do you want to see this gift used for the kingdom of Jesus?

2. How can I walk with you, learn from you, encourage you, and serve you during this time of generational tension?

3. What would it look like for the church to equip and use the gifts that your generation has to offer? What would it look like for members of your generation to belong in unity to the multigenerational body of Christ?

NOTE FROM GENERAL EDITOR
D. JAY MARTIN

O ver the last seven years my four children have all attended our local elementary school right down the road from our house. There's an old stone house that sits next to the school. The driveway to this home runs parallel to the main entrance of the school. Everyday hundreds of children ride to and from class, passing by the old home.

For several years, flying proudly from the front step, easily seen from the road, a political flag waved in the breeze, addressing our current president of the United States. The flag said . . . well, I can't publish the word printed alongside the name Biden. Unfortunately, I'm sure you can fill in the blank.

But that is the word that every child, every day, for multiple years was greeted with when entering or exiting the school grounds. What does this flag teach our children? It educates them in hatred, in disrespectful speech, and it teaches them to see those we disagree with, especially politically, as enemies.

Our children are inundated with similar messages daily. Christians have a unique opportunity to model for our children a better way. This is why I asked Connie Marchetti to write a children's lesson for **Before the Booth**. What follows is a creative way of telling our children who they are in Christ, and how we are to view others, even when we are different from one another.

THE KINGDOM WAY:
A CHILDREN'S LESSON
IN SPIRITUAL IDENTITY

CONNIE MARCHETTI

*Children's Ministry at Coventry Church & Director of
the English Program at Footprint Church*

D ID YOU KNOW YOU WERE created in the image of God? Did you know that every single person in the whole world is made in the image of God? He made you with his very own tender hands in your mom's belly. God made you because he loves you and he wants you to know about him and share that truth with others!

How cool would it be to get a letter from God? Well, I've been thinking about this quite a bit, and I think that if God the Father were to write you a personal letter from heaven, these are some of the things that I believe he would most want to say to you:

Dear Sweet Child,

IN JESUS YOU ARE FORGIVEN

I love you more than you can understand. I love you so much that I sent my Son Jesus to take your place on the cross to wash all your sins and mistakes away. When you trust my Son Jesus as your Savior and commit to following him, you get a brand-new heart! You are a new creation; you are given a new heart to help you love me with everything you have and love your neighbor as yourself.

Your new heart is being transformed to be like Jesus, the true King. As your heart is changed to be like Jesus' heart, you learn how to live in my kingdom following King Jesus. When you know I love you, and you love me back, even your thoughts, feelings, and actions will match my own. This kingdom way of living is the same as my Jesus' way of living. The opposite of the kingdom way is the way of the world. The way of the world may seem easy, but it leads to pain and hurt.

Key Scriptures:
(Matthew 22:37–39, Ezekiel 36:26)

YOU ARE A CHILD OF THE MOST-HIGH KING

Listen carefully because what I'm about to tell you is truer than anything that anyone will ever say about you. When you accepted my Son Jesus, you also became my beloved child! There is nothing that can snatch you from my hand. Nothing in all the world, anywhere, or anything will change my love for you that is found in Christ Jesus. I am and always will be your good Father. You are mine and I call you by my own name. You are my treasured and chosen child. And I deeply care about your friends, neighbors, and family members too! In fact, I want everyone in every part of the earth to know my love like this.

Key Scriptures:
  (1 John 3:1, Romans 8:38–39)

YOU ARE A KINGDOM CITIZEN

Do you remember the Lord's Prayer? In this prayer Jesus taught his followers to pray like this, "Your kingdom come, your will be done, on earth as in heaven."

When you trusted Jesus as your Savior and King, you became a child of my kingdom. Just like when a person who is a citizen of America is called an "American," you are a kingdom citizen and are called a "citizen of heaven." As a citizen of my kingdom, you will have the power of my Holy Spirit to help you be strong and brave. Everyone, everywhere on earth, who trusts in my Son Jesus is also a citizen of heaven.

Key Scriptures:
  (Matthew 6:10, Philippians 3:20–21)

YOU ARE LIGHT TO A DARK WORLD

When I made you, I placed some very special gifts inside of you. I did that for a reason. As you continue to follow me you will be filled up with my light and love. Because you are not a part of the kingdom of darkness, but of the kingdom of heaven, you are filled with my light. Where you go, I go, and where you walk, I walk with you. The Bible is my love story of your rescue and is designed to help guide your life. My Word is a lamp for your feet and a light for your path. Stay close to me and you will shine bright, able to light up everywhere you walk with my love and truth.

Key Scriptures:

(Ephesians 5:8–14, Psalm 119:105)

YOU ARE MY PRECIOUS SHEEP

I am your Gentle Shepherd, and you are my precious sheep. I am here to comfort you, rescue you, guide you, feed you, protect you, and carry you close to my heart. Oh, how much I love you. How deep and wide, full, and complete is my never ending, unconditional love for you!

Key Scriptures:

(Isaiah 40:11, Ephesians 3:18)

YOU ARE SAFE

Trust me and come to me with anything. I will never, ever leave you. When you feel sad or scared, come to me. I will help you. You do not need to be afraid because you are safe with me. No matter what happens in your life, keep looking to me. Like a tree with roots that grow deep down in the soil, when you choose to deepen your understanding of me, I will strengthen and make your faith firm. Your close relationship with me will help teach others to be citizens of heaven too.

Key Scriptures:

(Hebrews 12:2, Colossians 2:7)

GO AND SHARE

Because you are my child, you get to go and share the kingdom way with others. Go and spread the light of Christ that I have given you. Stay in my love.

You are free to love and serve me. As you follow me, you will learn more of my way of seeing and loving others. You can spread Jesus' love, his truth, and his life wherever you go. As a citizen of heaven, and my loved child, I want to teach you how to share my love with others!

Key Scriptures:

(John 15:9, John 14:6)

LET'S REVIEW

I am your Savior, Good Father, and King, Light in the dark, and your Gentle Shepherd. I desire what is best for you. When you pray to me, I always hear you. I love to hear you talk to me. Before you call, I will answer. I want you to trust me.

When you ask for something, I might say "yes," but sometimes I might say "no" (because I have something better), or I might say "not yet." Trust me more than your own ideas and I will show you the right way.

Keep walking in the kingdom way and invite others to walk with you! It will not always be easy, but I promise you it will be worth it. I love you forever and always!

Sincerely,
Your Good Father

Key Scriptures:

(Proverbs 3:5–6, Jeremiah 31:3)

SEVEN-DAY CHALLENGE TO PARENTS AND TEACHERS

This letter was specifically written with older-elementary-age children, third through sixth grades, in mind. Consider printing out the seven sections of the letter as seven letters that you give to your child over the course of a full week. Each day you can read the assigned section of the larger letter and the Scriptures referenced in that section.

DISCUSSION & REFLECTION

1. What does it mean that every person is "made in the image of God"?

2. How should this teach us to treat other people? What about people we don't necessarily like or agree with? Does God still care about them?

THE CHURCH ABOVE POLITICS

CHAD T. STOECKER

Lead Pastor at Mstar Church

DURING THE ELECTION CYCLE OF 2020, a member of the church I pastor shared with me, with both conviction and sincerity, "Pastor, if we don't win this election, the church is in trouble." My immediate response was very "Christian-y." "Hey, don't worry, God is still on the throne." But I walked away wrestling with several questions—the first being, *Does anyone really win in a national election?* The second, *Has our western cultural mindset led us to believe that the success of the church is dependent on variables other than Jesus?*

Can I ask you to wrestle through this important question with me: *Is the "success" of the church dependent on anything, or anyone, other than Jesus?*

Over the years, I've fielded some of the following comments and questions that touch this article's key question:

- "What do you think will happen to the church if Christians lose the privilege of deducting their charitable donations for tax purposes?"
- "The church's decline began when prayer was no longer allowed in schools."
- "For the church to succeed, we are going to have to get back to the principles this nation was founded on."

I enjoy and take advantage of tax credits for the tithes and offerings I give to the local church. And I would love for there to be prayer in school—and in homes, and in churches for that matter! And yes, I believe that a nation that honors the Word of God in its practices will be blessed by living out the will of God. But neither the Bible, nor church history, would agree that the success of the church is dependent on any of these temporal and earthly variables.

The first mention of the church—as we have come to understand it today—was by Jesus in Matthew 16:18. Jesus, speaking to his disciple Peter, said, "And I tell you that you are Peter, and on this rock I will build my church, and the gates of Hades will not overcome it." In this passage, Jesus informs his disciples that he will build his church on the foundation of Peter's confession. Peter's testimony back in verse 16 was this, "You are the Messiah, the Son of the living God." In the same conversation Jesus went on to assure the disciples that even though resistance to the church was going to be formidable, evil, relentless—and any of the other negative adjectives you can think of for the gates of Hades—these attempts would be futile to stop the plans of Jesus Christ for his church. Jesus is still building his church on the same testimony and confession today. Jesus is the Christ, the Son of the living God, and all authority in heaven and on earth belongs to him.

The birth of the church on the day of Pentecost, recorded in Acts 2, reveals how Christ's plan to build his church unfolded with perfection and precision. Throughout the book of Acts we continue to read of the incredible force that the church became as people from around the Roman Empire came to faith in the Lord. As individuals and families gave their allegiance to Christ, entire communities were turned upside down for Jesus. And all this happened not because government tax credits were given to the early church's donors, or because prayer was welcomed into pagan Roman schools, or even that Rome governed in a righteous manner. In fact, the opposite was taking place. Jews and Christians were severely taxed by the government. Jewish and Christian public prayer was, during times of persecution, punishable by death. During some of the worst persecutions, even private prayer gatherings discovered in house churches led to punishment. The Roman empire in the first century was one of the most pagan and heathen kingdoms the world has ever known.

What can we learn from this? The first century church of Jesus Christ did not thrive because of national freedoms, it thrived despite state-sponsored persecution! Why? Because the success of the church has always been based first in the faithfulness of Jesus, and then secondly founded upon the church's trust and allegiance to Jesus Christ.

Now back to our original question: *Is the success of the church dependent on anything, or anyone, other than Jesus?*

Absolutely not! The church is dependent on Christ alone.

I believe that the Western church has at times relied too heavily for her success on cultural and national variables, wandering from the simple truth that *Jesus builds his church!* Often, we have been tempted to place the success of the church under the umbrella of nationalism. We think that if the right people are elected, or if the right party is in office, or if the right laws are passed, then the church will succeed.

The wonderful truth is God himself is the umbrella under which everything in his creation resides. From the beginning of time, he has demonstrated his authority over all his creation. And let us not forget that God is the author and perfecter of our faith and the true builder and leader of the church.

God's plan for the Israelites living in Egypt was not subject to Pharaoh's authority or Egypt's laws. Nor was their safety contingent even on God's own natural law (a sea is not designed to part down the middle). The Hebrew boys' safety was not dependent on yielding to Nebuchadnezzar's authority, and because of God's intervention, their bodies were not consumed by the natural consequences of fire.

Likewise, the New Testament church, by all measures, should never have spread beyond Jerusalem. The church didn't have the support of the Jewish or Roman religious leaders. The church faced significant persecutions from hostile governments and was led by "unschooled, ordinary men" (Acts 4:13). There wasn't a seminary-trained leader among them! But what did they have? They had the promised Holy Spirit of Christ, who empowered them in ways far beyond their more "qualified" religious adversaries. All this took place within in a society determined to shut them down.

The results? "And the Lord added to their number daily those who were being saved" (Acts 2:47). Despite not having organized religion and political power on her side, the church became an unstoppable force—and because we serve the God who delivers us out of slavery, and parts the sea, and saves us from the fiery furnace, and guides us through seasons of hardship and persecution, the church is still unstoppable today!

Every four years I share this same message with my congregation. Routinely there are those who question me, asking if I am preaching "abstinence" when it comes to political involvement and voting. To this I respond: *No!* It is our right as American citizens to vote and to express biblical principles in the ballot box, or in public forums, or even as elected officials. This is one of the wonderful blessings of living in this incredible country, and we should take advantage of it.

However, it is our deeper responsibility as followers of Jesus to place all our trust in the Lord. This means believing that Jesus is in control even when we don't see it. This means loving those who don't agree with us even when we don't feel like it. This commitment to Jesus requires us to reach out to people with the gospel of Truth even when earthly authorities won't allow it. We live under the umbrella of American citizenship, and we must be law-abiding citizens to the best of our ability. But above the authority of our national government is God Almighty and he has a plan for his church to prosper even in the face of resistance and persecution. Under his authority we must be Spirit-led believers, first and foremost.

Yes, it is a blessing when earthly governments embrace the authority and plan of God Almighty. But as we have seen in both the New Testament, and throughout church history, the success of the church is not dependent on a political election or an earthly government. The success of the church is dependent on Christ alone. Our response to him must always be one of faith and allegiance.

DISCUSSION & REFLECTION

1. Is there a metric other than the faithfulness of Christ that you have been tempted to see as the measuring line of the church's "success"?

2. Can we still trust in the faithfulness and authority of Jesus even when it seems like things aren't going well in our nation?

3. What are ways that you see Jesus actively building his kingdom in your community?

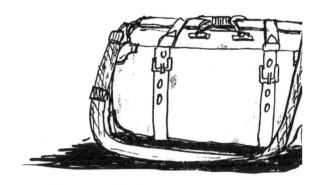

COMPETITOR, TOURIST, OR AMBASSADOR?

SCOTT NEWCOMER

Area Director for Christian Business Men's Connection

THIS ARTICLE IS DESIGNED FOR those that are Christ followers and are employed either part time or full time in the secular marketplace. The modern workplace can be a difficult realm to function as a Christian. Much of the challenge emerges from the desire or need to accomplish great things, or from performance-related issues. Add to this the upcoming election, and it's no wonder that emotions and stress can run rampant in the business world. You, like many others, may find yourself wishing for a spiritual GPS to help you navigate the landscape and find your way to your destination.

The key question is, "Who are you at your workplace?" How do you show up when you walk through the doors or log on to the video conference? What *persona* are you arriving with on Monday morning, and does it differ from the one you have on Sunday? Are you coming in Monday ready to conquer the world, ready to work "faithfully as onto the Lord," ready to "set the heathen straight," or are you living and working as an *ambassador for Jesus* in the marketplace? In this article I want to examine three personas that folks in the marketplace can adopt. These ways of approaching the business world can either help or hinder our witness as followers of Jesus. The three personas are *ambassador, tourist,* or *competitor.*

Let's start with encouragement from the Bible. What does Scripture reveal as our identity in Christ? If we are Spirit-filled Christ followers then our identity in him should influence and shape every sphere of our lives, including our workplaces. The apostle Paul wrote in 2 Corinthians 5:20 HCSB (emphasis added):

> Therefore, we are *ambassadors for Christ,* certain that God is appealing through us. We plead on Christ's behalf, "Be reconciled to God."

Scripture teaches that we *are* ambassadors. It does not say that we *should be* ambassadors. Rather, the Bible says that, as Christians, we *are* ambassadors for Christ.

What does it mean to be an *ambassador?* An ambassador is an official representative from one country, land, or kingdom sent to another country to represent their home nation or kingdom.

As born-again believers we are now citizens of heaven and ambassadors for Christ (Ephesians 2:19). As members of Jesus' kingdom, we are commissioned and sent as his ambassadors to represent the kingdom of God and embody God's desire to reconcile people to himself through Christ. This call is not just for Sunday mornings. It is a call to represent him wherever we go, whether we feel like it or not.

Another role that a person can have when they are traveling outside of their country, visiting another land, is that of a *tourist*. A tourist is someone visiting outside of their own country, but their purpose is to relax and enjoy themselves. As Christians, we should be asking ourselves, *Am I acting like an ambassador for Jesus or am I acting like a tourist in the way I conduct myself day to day?* A sobering point is that no matter how we are acting in the world, we are still an ambassador of the kingdom. We are ambassadors twenty-four hours a day, 365 days a year, always representing the culture and values of the King.

If our primary focus is getting ahead, and if our deepest values are shaped by making the most money, we are likely acting as another persona instead of ambassador.

A third persona that we can take on in the workplace is that of *competitor*.

It's very common to wear the colors or logo of our favorite sports team to work or around town on the weekends, and even to church on game day! For many folks it's innocent fun and sporting our team's jersey can help facilitate interesting conversations. But for others, perhaps someone who cheers for a rival team, wearing your team colors makes you the *enemy*. Life can quickly take on a zero-sum, winner-or-loser mentality.

I remember a time when the church leadership team I was serving on met during a big rivalry NFL game. The match was on the TV in a neighboring room. It was a big game between our local team, the Eagles, and their arch rivals, "America's Team." Within our church leadership team, we had fans of both NFL teams. At first our rivalry was handled with good-natured fun. But then we found ourselves not only rooting *for* our team, but *against* the other team. There was even cheering when players were injured!

I remember how quickly the love and good will of being on the same leadership team faded away and awkwardness and personal hurt crept in. In a moment of introspection, I was surprised to notice I was even having a hard time supporting the "other side's" ministry ideas! This all took place around *sports*. Things can get so much more heated around politics. What a tragedy it is when things like sports or partisan politics divide us and keep us from shining the light of the gospel of Jesus!

When I reflect on this situation, I notice how hurt I was by others cheering for my team's injuries. The same is true of partisan politics. When we turn the "other side" into the enemy, not only cheering for our team, but actively rooting for the downfall of the other team, we inadvertently turn those who support them into the enemy. Whether or not we agree with them, they likely have deeply personal reasons for why they vote the way they do. We can talk casually or intellectually about political topics and be callous about the personal implications concerning the issue to the other person, thereby alienating the person from us. This makes me wonder—if I say I care about you, but don't care about what you care about (or why you care about it), is that really caring about you?

Now, transfer this whole mindset to the upcoming elections. Our media seems to want to polarize the population. Which side are you on? Red or Blue? There are hardly any meaningful discussions about the pros and cons of a politician's actual ideas and policies. Instead, folks are forced to pick a side in entirety; Red *or* Blue. All too quickly those overly competitive juices get flowing. It's easy to make Red versus Blue, Republican versus Democrat, and the upcoming election into the big game. A competitive Super Bowl spirit starts to pervade the workplace. Will my guys or your guys win? Wearing political colors, slogans, phrases, or even politician names is swapped out for wearing our favorite team's jersey. The question then is how does this competitive spirit impact the willingness of others to listen to our ideas—whether work ideas, or worse yet, spiritual ideas?

As Christians in the marketplace, let's live out our real identity first and foremost, the identity that Scripture teaches and affirms. If we are in Christ, then we are an ambassador of Christ for reconciliation. Our primary calling is to promote the wonderful gift of Christ and the culture and values of love that the kingdom stands for, of which we are citizens. This identity is deeply connected to the Great Commission, where we are told to "go and make disciples." At CBMC we often say that for those working in the marketplace, their role is to be a "Marketplace Ambassador" for Christ, with a heart to tell people about the wonderful gospel, seeking to help others become disciples of Christ.

A problem arises when we also take on the Red or Blue identity. Instead of representing the kingdom of Jesus, we can start to be ambassadors of a Red or Blue worldview. It's a very subtle next step into the competitive mindset. We don't just cheer for our team to win, but then we also cheer for the other team and that team's supporters to lose.

This type of political competitiveness is so detrimental to our testimony to "love your neighbor as yourself" (Matthew 19:19). When the workplace environment breaks down into a competitive political atmosphere, how open is the other person going to be to anything you have to say about the gospel of Jesus? Is the competition of earthly partisan politics worth the destruction that can happen to our testimony?

I was recently at a social event where I was having a great conversation with a new Jewish friend. We were talking about life and the difficult situation and choices that Israel is currently facing. I asked him if he was a cultural Jew or only ethnically

Jewish? He said "both," and the discussion moved into some interesting biblical topics. Somehow Trump versus Biden came up. Statements were made as if they were fact that I didn't agree with, and I started to offer an alternate perspective. As we briefly debated, it hit me, which issue is more important here? Winning an argument about a political point? No! It was clear I was being presented with an option. I paused, stopped bringing alternative political points up, and steered the discussion back to faith and our mutual desire to know and love God.

How easy it can be to have more passion and energy, and maybe even love, for the Red team or the Blue team. Do we have more passion for a political team than for the One who died for us? Can the cheering for our political team here on earth even compare with the cheering in heaven for a lost soul that just gave their life to Christ?

Are we tourists just trying to have a good time and make a lot of money, competitors trying to win an earthly competition, or ambassadors representing the kingdom of Jesus? As Christians, we are told we are ambassadors. This is your mission. As you walk out your unique vocation and calling as a follower of Jesus in the secular marketplace, you are primarily called to be a Marketplace Ambassador for Christ and a citizen of the kingdom of Jesus.

DISCUSSION & REFLECTION

1. What identity or persona do you generally have when you're at work? Do those you work around know that you're a Christ follower and experience a connection between your walk and your talk that proves this?

2. As you were reading this article, did the Holy Spirit bring any situations, comments, or interactions with specific individuals to your mind? If so, what would God have you do as a response?

3. What changes to your morning preparation, your at-work heart attitude, or your definition of personal and career success would allow you to be a better ambassador for Christ in your workplace? Is there anything that is holding you back from making these changes?

4. If your coworkers knew of your political perspectives, would that make them more or less willing to hear about Jesus Christ from you? How should that then influence your conversations at work?

ABOUT THE CONTRIBUTORS

BRANDON BEST

Brandon Best serves as the Area Director for Young Life Tri-County (tricountypa.younglife.org). A buckeye living in Phoenixville with his wife (Faith), daughter (Florence), and son (Asa). He and Faith have been working with teenagers for fifteen years through Young Life, as a schoolteacher, a coach, and various ministry roles inside and outside the church. Brandon has his Master of Divinity through Westminster Theological Seminary and his bachelor's degree in math education from The Ohio State University. Over the past nineteen years Brandon has been seeking to live out resilient discipleship in his own life.

DARRELL C. BROWN JR.

Pastor Darrell Brown and his wife, Marian, have seven children and eighteen grandchildren. Darrell has been pastoring for ten years. He holds a Master of Theology through Slidell Baptist Seminary and is currently working toward his Doctorate degree. One of Darrell's greatest honors is being the founding pastor and serving the Pottstown area through Rhema Ministries International (rhemaministry.org).

DAISY COCAR

Daisy Cocar serves as the Program Director of Joann's Cottage, a Place of Hope program (placeofhope.com/maternity-care) and faith-based maternity group home for young mothers in foster care and their babies. She resides in West Palm Beach, Florida, with her husband and two cats and is a part of an active church community at Christ

Fellowship Church (christfellowship.church). Daisy also has the honor of serving the Phoenixville area through Footprint Church (freechristianellclass.com) located in Phoenixville, Pennsylvania, alongside her parents and founding Pastors Oscar and Melvi Cocar. Daisy is an alum of Cairn University where she received a Bachelor of Science in Bible and a Bachelor of Science in Social Work before being awarded a Master of Social Work from Bryn Mawr College.

TIM DOERING

Tim and his wife, Jen, live in Chester County. They have two young-adult sons. Tim pastored in local church ministry for eighteen years before transitioning into his current role, where he provides vision and teaching leadership of a cross-denominational network and unity movement called Netzer. *You can discover more about Netzer at Netzer.org, and you can hear more from Tim and others on Netzer's podcast,* The Quiet Reformation.

CORY ERMOLD

Cory Ermold is the Pastor of Worship and Creative Arts at Mstar Church (mstar.org) in Bechtelsville, Pennsylvania. He and his wife, Naomi, have two children. He enjoys a life of dedication and balance. Beyond his church responsibilities, Cory enjoys taking to the skies in powered paragliding, while his creative side finds expression in photography. These hobbies not only bring adventure but a different perspective to be experienced in daily life.

NOEL GENIZA

Pastor Noel Geniza was born in the Philippines and immigrated to the United States with his wife, Lani, in the '90s. Pastor Noel and Lani have three adult children who

134

*all participate in worship leading in their local church.
Pastor Noel is the founding pastor of International Christian
Fellowship (facebook.com/InternationalChristianFellowship)
in Pottstown, Pennsylvania.*

JESSE HOFFMAN

*Jesse Hoffman is a graduate of Lancaster Bible College
and serves as the Associate Pastor at Coventry Church in
Pottstown, Pennsylvania (coventrycob.org). He is married
to his lovely wife, Hannah, and they enjoy serving the Lord
alongside one another. Jesse leads the youth and young-adult
ministries at Coventry Church and helps oversee a variety of
aspects of the ministry.*

CONNIE MARCHETTI

*Mrs. Marchetti has been a lover of Jesus and a teacher of
children for many years. She lives with her husband, two
boys, and three dogs in Chester County, Pennsylvania.
She serves in children's ministry at Coventry Church
(coventrycob.org) in Pottstown and directs an English
Program at Footprint Church (freechristianellclass.com) in
Phoenixville.*

CHRIS McCARTY

*Chris McCarty is a local family physician who has practiced
in Southeastern Pennsylvania for the past decade. He grew
up in the Catholic Church; however, he started to form a
relationship with Jesus after meeting his wife, Natalie. In
2013, he grappled with the weight of his sin and gave his
life to Jesus. He is passionate about serving Jesus by helping
others in need. He lives near Pottstown, Pennsylvania, with
his wife and five children. He is a deacon at Parker Ford
Church (pfcchurch.com). As a physician, he is grateful to*

walk through his patients' lives with them and pray for them. He holds a Doctorate of Osteopathic Medicine from Philadelphia College of Osteopathic Medicine and a Master of Business Administration from Eastern University.

SCOTT NEWCOMER

Scott Newcomer has served as the MidAtlantic Area Director for CBMC, Christian Business Men's Connection, for the last eighteen years when God called him to step out of the Corporate world to go into full-time ministry. Scott worked for twenty years in the corporate world, in information technology for the health-care sector in roles in technology, leadership, and executive sales. Scott and Susan, his wife of thirty-six years, have two adult children, a daughter-in-law, and a new grandson. They also have two Rottweiler fur babies named Blue and Blossom.

CBMC is a nonprofit ministry stretching around the globe that focuses on presenting Jesus in the marketplace and helping men grow to be the men God designed them to be. For more info check out CBMC.com.

JOSH PARK

Josh Park, a founding pastor of Branch Life Church (branchlife.church) serving the greater Pottstown area, established the Ashwood Apartment fire relief center (2020) and served on the community response teams for Hurricane Ida (2021) and the Pottstown home explosion (2022). These efforts and more have led to the establishment of the Life Crisis Response and Counseling Center, coming in 2024 / 2025.

TERRANCE PAUL

Pastor Terrance Paul is originally from the beautiful islands of Trinidad and Tobago. With a heart for serving God and guiding others on their faith journey, Pastor Terrance has dedicated his life to ministry. Married to his loving wife, Margaret, for thirty years, they have built a strong and supportive partnership in both their personal and spiritual lives. Together, they have raised two wonderful adult children and are blessed with two adorable grandchildren.

As the Senior Pastor of Fresh Start Ministries International (fsministries.org), Pastor Terrance provides guidance, inspiration, and support to his congregation. Outside of his pastoral duties, Pastor Terrance also serves as the CEO of Fresh Start Learning Center, a child care facility that will open its doors in September 2024. In addition, Pastor Terrance is eagerly preparing for the launch of his upcoming Fresh Talk *podcast, set to debut in August 2024. Through this platform, he aims to engage listeners in meaningful conversations, exploring various topics related to faith, personal growth, and everyday life.*

REGAN SIGOURNEY

Regan Sigourney is a member of Gen Z and a special education teacher with a Master's degree in Trauma Informed Education. Regan helps offer spiritual leadership at Chesmont Young Adults, a regional ministry for young adults across the Chester and Montgomery County areas. She also serves in youth ministry at Parker Ford Church (pfcchurch.com).

CHAD T. STOECKER

Chad T. Stoecker is the Lead Pastor at Mstar Church (mstar.org). He's been an ordained minister with the Assemblies of God since 2000. He's married to Michelle, and this year they celebrate their thirtieth wedding anniversary. They have three grown children: Chad Ryan (28), Cole (25), and Kacey (20).

JOE TERRERI

Joe is the Lead Pastor of Connection Church in Pottstown, Pennsylvania (cometoconnect.com), where he has served for seventeen years. He has been married to his wife, Cheryl, for twenty years, and they have four children: Joseph, Lucy, Olivia, and Ezra. Joe enjoys cooking, golfing, and reading. He is a loyal yet discouraged fan of the Buffalo Bills.

JUSTIN VALENTINE

Pastor Justin Valentine is the Senior Pastor of Kingdom Life Church (klcnow.org) in Pottstown, Pennsylvania. He has been preaching the gospel for over twenty-five years and has a passion to see lives changed by the power of God. Pastor Valentine is married to his beautiful wife, Antoinette, and has five children and two grandchildren.

ABOUT THE ARTIST

SHANNON VINING

Shannon Vining is a wife, mom of seven, poet, pianist, artist, and singer-songwriter. She is the Director of Creative Arts at Parker Ford Church (pfcchurch.com). You can find her music on Spotify/YouTube/iTunes (under her name), and her illustrated poetry on Instagram and Facebook @Crownofstormspoetry.

NOTES

ONE THING

1. H.B. Charles Jr., "The Supremacy of Jesus Christ," *Hbcharlesjr.com*, December 7, 2017, https://hbcharlesjr. com/wp-content/uploads/2017/11/The-Supremacy-of-Jesus-Christ-2017.pdf.

WHAT YOUR BODY IS SAYING ABOUT THIS ELECTION

1. Andrew Dugan, "Serious Depression, Anxiety Affect Nearly 4 in 10 Worldwide," *Gallup*, October 20, 2021, https:// news.gallup.com/opinion/gallup/356261/serious-depression-anxiety-affect-nearly-worldwide.aspx.

2. Jacob Westfall, Leaf Van Boven, John Chambers, and Charles Judd, "Perceiving Political Polarization in the United States: Party Identity Strength and Attitude Extremity Exacerbate the Perceived Partisan Divide," *Perspectives on Psychological Science,* 2015.

3. Sameera Nayak, Timothy Fraser, Panagopoulos, and Daniel Kim, "Is Divisive Politics Making Americans Sick? Associations of Perceived Partisan Polarization with Physical and Mental Health Outcomes Among Adults in the United States." *Social Science and Medicine,* 2021.

4. Brett Ford, Matthew Feinberg, Bethany Lassetter, Sabrina Thai, and Arasteh Gatchpazain, "The Political Is Personal: The Costs of Daily Politics." *Journal of Personality and Social Psychology: Attitudes and Social Cognition,* 2023.

BEST PRACTICES FOR SOCIAL MEDIA USAGE DURING THE ELECTION CYCLE

1. Greg McFarlane, "How Facebook (meta), X Corp (twitter), Social Media Make Money From You," *Investopedia,* December 2, 2022, https://www.investopedia.com/

stock-analysis/032114/how-facebook-twitter-social-media-make-money-you-twtr-lnkd-fb-goog.aspx.

2. Ally Daskalopoulos, Nadia Hernandez, Felix Jason, Holly Jenvey, David Gustafson, Robin Mosley, Cam Rodriguez, Nika Schoonover, and Sitoria Townsend, "Thinking Outside the Bubble: Addressing Polarization and Disinformation on Social Media," *CSIS Journalism Bootcamp,* September 27, 2021, https://journalism.csis.org/thinking-outside-the-bubble-addressing-polarization-and-disinformation-on-social-media/.

ORIENTING TO JESUS IN THE TENSION

1. C.S. Lewis, "Learning in War-Time," *The Weight of Glory and Other Addresses* (HarperSanFrancisco, 1980), pp. 59-61.

2. Steve K. Jablonski, "Epilogue," (New Line Music Corp.), 2011.

3. Alain Albert Boublil, Claude Michel Schonberg, Herbert Kretzmer, Jean Marc Natel, "Do You Hear the People Sing?", (Warner Chappell Music, Inc.), 1980.

DEAR GEN Z, BOOMERS, & EVERYONE IN-BETWEEN

1. Marc Freedman, Eunice Lin Nichols, "Is America Ready to Unleash A Multigenerational Force for Good?" *Encore.org,* 2022, https://cogenerate.org/wp-content/uploads/2022/09/Encore-Cogneration-Report-1.pdf.

2. Brian Johnson, Phil Wickham, Bill Johnson, Chris Davenport, "Hymn of Heaven," (Be Essential Songs), 2021.

ACKNOWLEDGMENTS

A COLLABORATIVE PROJECT LIKE THIS IS only possible through teamwork and selflessness. I want to thank all the contributors and the ministries and churches they represent. Any proceeds generated from this book are being donated to organizations working with underserved youth in Pottstown, Pennsylvania. Each of the contributors participated in this book because they agree that the American church needs a better, more Christlike approach to navigating partisan politics. Thank you for believing in that vision.

This book would not have happened without the support of my wife, Julie, or of the Parker Ford Church leadership and staff. Thank you for empowering me to go after these sorts of unique ministry projects. Thanks to our featured artist, Shannon Vining, who dedicated many hours to reading, praying through, and creating original art pieces for each chapter. The book is so much better for this beautiful artistic touch. Connection Church was also crucial in the development of the book. Thank you, Pastor Joe Terreri and Connection leadership, for your partnership and support. Joe got me connected with our publisher, Debbie Capeci at Morning Joy Media. Working with Debbie has been an amazing experience. Thank you, Debbie!

Lastly, thank you to Netzer. Netzer's vision for church unity has shaped my pastoral imagination in countless ways. Tim Doering and Brandon Hanks helped me read and think critically through each of the book's essays. I needed their help to make sure everything we published was faithful to basic Christian orthodoxy and was spiritually edifying to the church. Thank you to Justin Boyer from Netzer who helped me produce a seven-part *Before the Booth* podcast series, released in the summer of 2024. You can listen to those episodes on Netzer's podcast, *The Quiet Reformation*.

—**D. Jay Martin**